Spirit
of the Shuar

Spirit of the Shuar

Wisdom from the Last Unconquered People of the Amazon

John Perkins
and
Shakaim Mariano Shakai Ijisam Chumpi

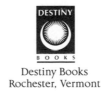

Destiny Books
Rochester, Vermont

Destiny Books
One Park Street
Rochester, Vermont 05767
www.InnerTraditions.com

Destiny Books is a division of Inner Traditions International

Library of Congress Cataloging-in-Publication Data
Perkins, John.
      Spirit of the Shuar : wisdom from the last unconquered people of the
Amazon / John Perkins and Shakaim Mariano Shakai Ijisam Chumpi.
            p.   cm.
      ISBN 0-89281-865-4 (pbk.)
      1. Shuar Indians—Religion. 2. Shuar philosophy. 3. Shamanism. I. Title.
F3722.1.J5 P46 2001
306' .089'98372—dc21

                                                                    2001002721

Printed and bound in Canada

10 9 8 7 6 5 4 3 2 1

Text design and layout by Rachel Goldenberg

This book was typeset in Aries with Bell Gothic as the display typeface

Contents

Acknowledgments

We thank all the Shuar for making this book possible, and especially those who live along the Mangosiza River, in and around the area known today as Miazal. There are many of you whose names are not included but who played vital roles: you listened to the stories; shared families, music, dances, and chicha; welcomed Dream Change Coalition (DCC) visitors; carried their packs; maneuvered their canoes through the rapids; helped them trek to the thermal waterfalls; and opened homes and hearts so generously to them.

We also thank those DCC visitors who journeyed far in order to learn from the Shuar and who now are helping to share the wisdom of the elders, inspiring dreams of a world that is sustainable and human societies that nurture the plants, animals, rivers, and mountains, as well as people. There are many of you too whose names are not mentioned in these pages but who are an integral part of the story. You know who you are; we honor you.

We thank Tsunkqui, Nunqui, Etsaa, Ayumpum, Jempe, and all the other spirits who bring wisdom to the Shuar. And the birds, insects, fish, animals, the plants and rocks, mountains and rivers—all that we have been and will become in other lives, our sisters and brothers, fathers and mothers.

This book would never have appeared in print had it not been for John's father, Jason Perkins, and daughter, Jessica, who accepted the daunting jobs of translating and typing the interviews Mariano conducted. When no one else was there and funding had run out, you persevered. We are deeply grateful for your generosity, talent, and dedication to this task.

Once the book was compiled, editor Elaine Sanborn stepped in to reorganize it. She immediately understood its weaknesses and set out to correct them. Although she has not visited the Shuar (yet!), she had a profound appreciation for the richness of their oral traditions. Masterfully she reworked the fabric, weaving it into a tapestry that—in context as well as content—reflects those traditions. We thank her from the bottom of our hearts.

Prologue

My name is Shakaim Mariano Shakai Ijisam Chumpi. I am Shuar. Like all my ancestors before me, I grew up in the Amazon jungle, learning to hunt wild boar and many other animals with a spear and blowgun and to kill the men who are our enemies. We Shuar are the best hunters and the bravest warriors in the entire world. It's our tradition to shrink the heads of our slain enemies. We've never been defeated and have never signed a peace treaty—not with the Incas, the Spaniards, or the governments of Ecuador, Peru, or the United States. The missionaries tell us that we are the only tribe in all the Americas who have never surrendered to anyone.

Unlike my parents, I attended Catholic mission school, where I learned to speak and read Spanish. Like most Shuar who are alive today, I have a Spanish name, Mariano. My first name—my Shuar name—Shakaim, means "Spirit of the Forest." I'm an expert shot with a rifle and have fought for the Ecuadorian army against the Peruvians; with two thousand other Shuar warriors of the Arutam brigade, I led the jungle war against Peru in 1995. Together we fought like our fathers, without mercy, valiantly. Many of my Shuar brothers died, but we killed more of our enemies. I carry tattoos on my body to prove it—but we Shuar never brag about the enemies we've killed or *tsantsas* [shrunken heads of enemies] we've taken! We know it's the power of *arutam* that made it possible.

Though most people today might not agree, we know that war is necessary if the jungle is to live in peace and thrive. The old shaman Chumpi used to teach us that men have a responsibility to make sure that peace includes all the plants, animals, rivers, and insects. Peace without peace for all is not true peace. Sometimes war is necessary to keep human populations in check, to maintain balance. We must protect all future generations, including those of the "others," the ones we eventually shapeshift into.

So it is important for us to possess arutam—both our men and women—in order to be effective hunters and warriors, parents, gardeners, and shamans and to pass this beautiful life on to future generations. Our ancestors created arutam when they died and transformed themselves into powerful animals. Its magic is carried in the forests, the sacred waterfalls, and the teacher plants—ayahuasca, datura, and wild tobacco. People who have arutam sometimes shapeshift into the anaconda or the jaguar and are able to overcome all obstacles. I come from a long line of ancestors with arutam.

I am twenty-six years old, the son of Domingo Chumpi and nephew of the famous shaman Chumpi (he had no Spanish name). My wife is Ujukam Kasent Nupirat Maria—Maria is her Spanish name. She is almost five years younger than I am. Like her ancestors, she grew up in the jungle, learning about the plants that our family needs for food and medicines, about taking care of children and training the hunting dogs. She also learned to make chicha, our most important food, a sacred and delicious beer that only women produce by preparing the manioc root in a special process, then chewing and spitting it into a large pot to ferment. Everyone around agrees that Maria makes the very best chicha! According to tradition, men aren't allowed to touch chicha with any part of our outside bodies except our mouths. Only women can make and touch it.

We Shuar know that men and women are equal but different. Men cut trees for building homes and dugout canoes, hunt animals for protein, and kill other men when it's necessary. Women tend the gardens and collect plants in the forests, raise children, make chicha, and—according to them—carry out the most important job of all: convincing us men to stop cutting trees, hunting animals, and killing enemies. When enough of this has been done, they might say, "Our house is too large already," or "Don't go hunting today; we've eaten enough meat this week." We men laugh about this. "Stay home and make love today," they say. We obey.

In the old days, those of our parents, there were many more women than men because of the headhunting wars. Due to their different jobs, men and women never live without each other. Therefore, one man might have two, three, or even four wives. If my uncle was killed in battle, his wives would go to live with my father. The women, though, had their own privileges, like teaching the young, uninitiated males the techniques for pleasing a woman in lovemaking. A woman also had the right to leave a man's house and her marriage to him—she simply walked away—but a man couldn't abandon a woman.

Now things are different. I have one wife and won't take another. Maria and I have four children. The first is our six-year-old daughter, Ujukam Zoila Pascualina Chumpi. She attends the mission school. The next is a son, Ujukam Wainchatai Mariano Chumpi. He is the godson of my friend and *amikri*, John Perkins. The next is Johnny, named after my amikri. Our youngest girl is named after my amikri's daughter, Jessica, who has come here to visit us. We live in Tsuirim (nowadays often called Miazal), in a traditional Shuar longhouse near my mother and father's home and close to my brothers. We've lived here for years and years, long before Juan Arcos and Padre Raul came to establish the mission and the school.

I tell you all this, talking into the tape recorder, because my amikri has asked me to and because I want to preserve the stories and traditions of my people. We say that *amikri* is the same as the Spanish word *compadre*, that John is the godfather of my son, Mariano; but in fact *amikri* means much more than that. It involves a sacred trust. In any case, John gave me this tape recorder, along with many cassettes and batteries, and asked me to interview my parents and the other old people among us in our own language, which we call Shuar, and which I later translated into Spanish. John said we could talk about anything; I could share my own feelings and impressions and those of my wife, Maria, and others our age, as well as those of the elders, the *uwishin*, the ones who know.

I was raised as a traditional Shuar, yet so much is changing around us. I've mentioned some of this already, but there's more. I'll tell you—or the older people who speak through me will—about the love lives of our people; the way we're initiated into adulthood; the coming of the missionaries and schools; the sacred medicine plants—ayahuasca, tobacco, and datura; the vision quests; the wars and how they help create peace; the spirits who teach us about the world and protect us and the trees and animals. We'll tell you how it was in the past and how it is now. According to what my father says, even though there was no mission and no school, his early life was much the same as my own. Now, though, things are really beginning to change.

John says it's important to share our knowledge with the rest of the world because our ways may help other people, his people in the North, to better understand the importance of the plants and animals and the ways we live with them. He says his people are in trouble and need our help. I believe him. He's brought North Americans and Europeans to visit us, and I've seen among them a lack of knowledge about the world and a hunger to understand. Maria and I have invited these people to our home and have been saddened to see how little they have. We Shuar are taught to read people, to look beyond their smiles. We can look at the gringos and see that they lack the fire that burns in the hearts of our people. They're longing for love. So I believe what John tells me, and, since he is my amikri—the most important relationship two Shuar men can share—I honor his request.

But I too have my reasons for making these tapes: my four children and the six who are yet unborn that Maria and I shall raise, and all their children, and their children's children, and the ones who come after that. For their sake, I asked John to make tapes as well and to write in the book that will grow from the tapes the story of how he came to know and love the Shuar, to be like one of us, to become my amikri. He lived among us before I was born and then returned when I had just become a teenager. After this he wrote an important book about us, which I read in Spanish, and then later brought his friend, the publisher of that book, to visit us, a man who dreamed this dream of giving me a tape recorder so I could save the history, stories, and traditions of the Shuar. I asked my amikri to include these things in his new book because they are part of the story, roots to the tree that is spreading its branches to the sons and daughters of our sons and daughters.

So, along with my amikri, I make these tapes for Pascualina, Mariano, Johnny, my Jessica, his Jessica, and all their children, and for the children of the trees, the fish, the birds, and the animals.

And for you, that you may learn to love the way we Shuar love, to be one with the world that is one with you.

Publisher's Preface

"Cholera!"

The headline on the front page of the *Wall Street Journal* advised travelers to avoid Ecuador because a cholera epidemic had broken out—an extremely unusual occurrence. There was no indication of when it would be over and if, in fact, it would be contained. My plane left for the capital city of Quito in five hours. What to do?

John Perkins, one of our authors, was expecting me in Miazal, Shuar Territory, Amazon. I had promised to come to meet with the Shuar provided I could be helpful in extending John's work. I figured the cholera would not be a problem if I limited my stay in Quito to just one night, being careful to eat only cooked foods. Then I could drive to Shell, the oil company town and military airstrip at the outskirts of the jungle, and leave "civilization" within two days. I felt confident that once I was in the jungle where the disease had not traveled, the dangers, both visible and invisible, would be ones I was prepared to meet. I headed for the Boston airport resolute, all sense of fear and foreboding driven from my consciousness. I was on my way to meet my friends, the Shuar.

The plane journey was uneventful. On my way through Quito customs and immigration, I grabbed the local newspaper and slipped it into the webbing of my knapsack. In the bag were all my possessions for this trip: camera, bedding, water purifier, notebook, two changes of clothing, a small Hi-8 camcorder, and a recently released, first-of-its-kind, compact digital tape recorder.

I was happy to get into my room. Before collapsing onto the bed, I dropped my knapsack and removed the newspaper. "War Breaks Out in the Disputed Territory: President of Ecuador to Meet with President of Peru Tomorrow to Try to Resolve Crisis." I just couldn't believe it. First cholera, now war? I was leaving for the so-called disputed territory tomorrow. It was a curious name, for as far as the Shuar were concerned, there was no dispute—it was their land, the wild and unconquered Upper Amazon Basin where they had lived since the first day.

The Shuar had never been conquered—not by the Incas, not by the Spanish Conquistadors, or the modern armies of cattle ranchers, gold miners, and oil companies. During World War II, however, the United States and Peru cut a deal, and a big chunk of Ecuador—Shuar land—was formally recognized as Peru. Of course, the Ecuadorians and the Shuar weren't in on the deal. To mark the border, the Peruvians simply dropped concrete blocks from airplanes onto a jungle they had never seen. Both the Ecuadorian and Peruvian armies had set up outposts at the fringes of Shuar land. For years there had been the occasional skirmish and now, war! Had I made a big mistake? Time to turn around? Get out? I decided to sleep on it.

I woke up in the morning refreshed and ready to travel. Then all the news of the day before flooded into my mind. I knew I couldn't reach John and I was also well aware that no one understood what was actually going on in Miazal. I also had no way of finding out what lay in my way between Quito and the Shell airstrip. I was confident that if I could get to Miazal, the fighting would be farther downriver and the Shuar would know exactly what was going on. I thought of the young Shuar warriors who had never shrunk a head, who had been to mission school and now spoke some Spanish—what would they think of this war?

I decided to make the journey. My Jeep and driver arrived as scheduled at 8:00 A.M. and I was off to the Amazon Basin, what the Ecuadorians refer to as the Oriente (East). Traveling this road from Quito on the Andean plateau, up to the continental divide at 13,000 feet, and down through all the climatic zones from alpine to jungle, was also a trip through the five-hundred-year history of colonization. From the International-style high-rise apartment buildings of Quito to the thatched huts surrounding the airstrip could be read the story of all the abuses and destruction that European culture had brought. Yes, there was progress, but more evident were poverty and the eradication and homogenization of cultures and languages. Ecuador was 40 percent indigenous and these peoples had suffered greatly. Vibrant cultures and communities had been reduced to shanty towns and the hope of the better life that could be seen on the satellite dish.

Suddenly the Jeep came to a screeching halt. Two Ecuadorian soldiers with machine guns motioned me out of the car. This was the border of the Oriente, a border within borders. No one was allowed into the Amazon jungle or out of it without military clearance. I could tell that the rotund sergeant was feeling very full of himself—after all, the country was in crisis and he had authority over me. Thoughts raced through my mind as I handed him my passport and he started giving my driver a hard time in Spanish. I restrained my desire to assert myself and let the game play out between the two of them. My driver was actually an ornithologist who had given up teaching about birds because he could make more money as a driver than he could as a professor. He was an Ecuadorian, a proud and highly intelligent man who spoke English, and I had enjoyed his commentary as we descended into the jungle.

He now assumed a very subservient body posture and spoke sweetly to the sergeant, telling him, in the little Spanish I could comprehend, how essential his role was and that he was taking this American publisher into the jungle to meet with colleagues on very important work. However, this work was in no way as significant as what the sergeant was now required to do for the honor and glory of his country. This flattery, plus fifty dollars, opened the gateway to the Oriente. We were off.

I arrived at the airstrip just as the pilot was taxiing his single-prop four-seater to the small hut that served as our waiting lounge. The plane had been in the service of Italian missionaries for some twenty years now. These missionaries would sometimes allow John to use their aircraft to get in and out of the jungle. This was, in fact, the only way to get back and forth since there were no roads and the trip by foot and canoe could take several weeks. The pilot, an old friend named Gustavo, assured me that John and everyone in Miazal were fine. However, many of the young Shuar warriors had been recruited by the Ecuadorian army and were now carrying AK-47s.

I climbed into the plane and we headed up through the ever-present rain clouds, over a vast area of elaborate river systems that snaked through the dense jungle, and finally down to a small dirt strip just barely visible through the trees. In the Upper Amazon it is extremely difficult to find a hundred yards of land with no water cutting through it. This was the only spot for miles around, and as we bounced along the rutted field I had to marvel at the skills and courage of pilots like Gustavo.

When it seemed that we had run out of land and would nose-dive into the river, the plane jerked to a stop. I thanked Gustavo and hurried to climb out over the wing. The sun was scorching. Immediately I was surrounded by Shuar warriors. Thanks to John they were expecting me. Several recognized me from my previous trip and shook my hand vigorously. They hustled me along a narrow trail to the river where a dugout canoe awaited us, then down-river to the community of Miazal.

John was standing on the riverbank. Next to him was Shakaim Mariano. I was relieved to see them and was reminded of the special relationship John has enjoyed with the Shuar since the 1960s—the way they treat him as a member of the tribe. Soon we were excitedly exchanging stories. John told me that many of the young men were gone and reports were coming back from the fighting that Peruvian heads had been taken.

Traditionally, in order for a Shuar male to become a warrior, he must kill an enemy and shrink his head. This is a rite of passage. The war in the jungle was a boon to these young men—they could now take heads and build up arutam, the vital force in Shuar culture that enables a man to succeed as a warrior, husband, and father and a woman to excel in her duties as a mother and wife. So rather than it being a sad, depressing, lamenting scene in Miazal, it was life as usual in the jungle, with the young men exhibiting their prowess and gaining a reputation worthy of marriage to the most prized young women.

John, along with Juan Gabriel, his Ecuadorian partner, had made all the arrangements. We were to set off in the morning to spend the night with Tuntuam, an elder shaman who had moved back to the area after many years of absence. I was particularly interested in seeing him because I was suffering from a severe GI-tract disturbance I had picked up earlier that year in India and simply had been unable to shake. I had tried homeopathy, herbal medicine, fasting, acupuncture, Chinese medicine, and even a course of antibiotics—my first in twenty years—all to no avail.

Early in the morning we arose and piled into the dugout canoes. The swollen river was treacherous, but the Shuar warriors stood in each canoe, one in the bow, another in the stern, skillfully maneuvering us through the rapids with long poles and paddles shaped like giant palm leaves. Eventually we passed fish traps that are typical of the Shuar and knew that Tuntuam's house was nearby. To the right was a small shingle of beach next to an out-cropping of land. A simple log raft had been pulled onto the sand. After we tied up alongside it we rested and watched a flock of parrots fly by, then John made the obligatory announcement calls—shrieks through the jungle—which were returned. Tuntuam's son was now standing at the top of the outcropping and could see us below. He motioned for us to follow him.

As we reached the top, we saw a rather new longhouse that his father had built. The son signaled us to enter. Sitting on a small turtle stool with his back against the central pillar of the house was Tuntuam. Beautiful feath-ers that adorned his head and a simple loincloth were his only garments. He and his wife performed a welcoming dance and asked us to be comfort-able and share their chicha, a traditional fermented beverage. Tuntuam's son had been educated by the missionaries, who had discouraged him from taking up his father's vocation. However, seeing that John and I were so interested and communicative with his dad, we later found out, gave him much to think about. Tuntuam and his wife, unlike his son, had the full tattooed markings of their clan. They would be known for who they were—the people, the Shuar.

That night we would drink *natem,* the vine of death, the vine of com-munion. *Natem* is Shuar for the plant that is known as ayahuasca to the Quechuas in the Andes. I told Tuntuam about the Battle of Bharat that was taking place in my stomach and he said he would help; he would definitely cure me. I asked Tuntuam if I could video the preparation of this divine substance and he agreed, actually feeling quite proud that I took such an interest in what was for him a basic means of personal development and education. He escorted us to the back of his longhouse and pointed to a vine, about two inches in diameter, snaking through the forest, weaving in and out among the trees. He told me how, twenty years ago when he had abandoned this site and moved upriver, he had planted the natem, knowing he would return someday after the jungle had taken over his small agricultural plot and restored it to its original nature. This was the way of the Shuar—hunting, gathering, farming on a small scale, and then moving on to new hunting grounds, allowing the land to replenish itself.

He cut the natem vine and gathered some leaves from a few neighboring plants. These were brought into the longhouse. His wife had already prepared a pot and was boiling water. Tuntuam removed the bark from the vine, chopped it into small pieces and added it to the water, along with the leaves. This would now boil and simmer for hours while we sat and drank more chicha and listened to songs and stories.

The coming of darkness is a magical experience in the jungle, ushered in by a rush of vibrant colors and an absolute racket in the canopy as the birds and other animals settle down for the night. Now all that could be seen in the sky were the stars. Tuntuam said the natem was ready and the moment was right. He drank down a cup of the vine of communion, followed by a bolt of 100 proof sugar-cane liquor to wash the very bitter taste out of his mouth, and started playing on his mouth harp, the *tumank*. This was the practice of the Shuar shaman—to journey and heal others under the influence of natem.

Tuntuam told me that he would look into my body and see what spirits were troubling it. Before he asked me to lie down on a bench, he offered me a cup of his elixir. I couldn't imagine rejecting his shamanic offering and drank the bitter brew without hesitation—or reflection, for that matter. I lay down and Tuntuam started chanting. Slowly the natem took hold and I was transported. The shaman could see some spirits had attached themselves to my stomach and were troubling me. He took his magic darts and banished them.

I got up from the bench and because the earth floor had not been completely finished in the new residence, sat on a leaf mat next to John. Tuntuam picked up his harp again and started playing. The ayahuasca enhanced and magnified for me the sounds of the music.

But the magic of the moment was violently interrupted by an incredible urge rushing through my body. Tuntuam could sense this and laughed while I headed for the door. John looked concerned and said, "Where are you going? Do you need to vomit?" Typically, when one takes ayahuasca, vomiting occurs before any other experience. In my case, which I later learned was more spiritual, things headed in the opposite direction. I was now in a mad dash, John yelling behind me, quite disturbed, "Wait! Wait!" I yelled back, "I'm okay—I'm just going to the river."

The river was a fury rushing by the small beach. I couldn't just step into the water—there might be piranha or an anaconda swimming by. I was amazed at my night vision, another effect of the natem, as my eye spotted in the pitch darkness a bend of tree root that had been exposed by the fast-moving current. I planted my feet firmly on the bank, grabbed the root, and stuck my biscuits in the wind. Soon the whole experience had been whisked down the river and I felt great. Tuntuam's medicine had cured me.

▲

The next day we headed back to Miazal to meet up with Yajanua Maria Arcos before moving on to visit Tukupi, an elderly Shuar warrior who lived still farther into the jungle—surrounded by the Achuar, traditional enemies of the Shuar—in an area named after him in honor of his stature. Maria was the daughter of don Juan Arcos, a deacon in the Catholic Church who was of Spanish descent, and Amalia Tuitsa, a full-blooded Shuar who was greatly respected as an herbal healer and shaman. Maria had studied at the mission school and later was one of the few Shuar to leave the jungle for further education in Quito. She had become a registered nurse and had grown away from the ways of the Shuar. After a profound experience with datura, a teacher plant sacred to her people, Maria returned to the way of her ancestors. The jungle spoke to her and she has listened ever since.

We met Maria just before we reached the airstrip. She was very excited to accompany John, whom she had known for years, and to be going to visit her old friend Tukupi. This famous warrior, now in his eighties or early nineties, was reputed to have taken more than thirty heads; most of the neighboring clans had lost a relative to him, though the clan warfare in the jungle had reached its apex some thirty years earlier and was now all but over.

The plane landed on a small dirt strip near Tukupi's longhouse. Maria, John, Juan Gabriel, and I made our way along the jungle path, giving out the traditional Shuar call as soon as we were in view of the dwelling. Children raced around the longhouse and two women worked the yucca gardens, but there was no sign of Tukupi. He was, we were informed, down at the river, bathing.

We headed in that direction. But before we reached the bend in the trail just ahead of the river's edge, Tukupi appeared. He stood tall and upright, naked except for a loincloth and a shotgun. Now an uwishin elder, he had long since given up the habit of carrying a man-killing spear hand-carved from the wood of the *chonta* tree. Maria and Tukupi were very happy to see each other. I knew that we were the first whites to be received by him in years, other than a missionary, and I felt relieved by the warm welcome. He had stopped headhunting and now was a highly regarded shaman, with both Shuar and Achuar coming to him for healings from deep in the jungle.

Tukupi asked us to join him in his longhouse for chicha. His two young wives busily arranged the turtle stools and stirred the beer. He explained that he once had four wives who all lived together. The other two, who had since died, were former wives of his brother and had come to him because his brother was killed in the wars. The six children in the longhouse—from ages three to fifteen—were the children of Tukupi and the two younger wives who had been "grown" by him, supported and cared for as his own children from the time when they were young to their initiation into adulthood, when they became his wives. He explained that this practice was common among the Shuar. A girl child would be married off to a great warrior at the age of seven or eight. The warrior performed all the functions of a father for this child until she reached puberty, at which time an initiation would take place and the marriage would be consummated. In this way the love of a daughter for a father would be transformed, once the child had grown, into the love of a woman for a man. The absence of blood ties meant that the two could have healthy children together.

I reflected on this extraordinary cultural arrangement—one that would be highly destructive in our culture—and how it had been channeled in a way that seemed to bring happiness and stability to the family. Like all cultural modalities, it had the potential for abuse as well as benefit. What I witnessed among the Shuar that night was a very positive family environment. Tukupi's two younger wives seemed genuinely happy, well adjusted, and affectionate toward him.

After his invitation to us to spend the night in his home, I asked if he was comfortable having our conversations recorded on tape. He smiled broadly, set his shotgun down on the bed, and handed an old spear to one of his grandsons. The young man helped me plant the spear into the ground; I set up my digital tape recorder, attached my microphone to the spear, and hit "record."

Night descended and the stories began, tales of his encounters with Achuar enemies. I asked how he could live on his own, surrounded by Achuar rivals, many of whom had lost members of their families to him. He told us that likewise several of his brothers and sisters and their spouses were killed during the wars, which ended in the late 1960s. With an impish grin he said that the Achuar used to send messages to him, taunting that he was weak, that he spent all his time making love with his wives and snorting tobacco. He always responded that he would prove this untrue, that he would show his arutam to any who cared to test him. He invited these Achuar to come and duel him to the death.

By firelight, Tukupi told us how he had taken the head of a neighbor's adult son, a man he saw as an enemy, sewed the eyes, nose and lips closed, shrunk it, and kept it with his many other heads. These were the source of his warrior power, his arutam, and he would never divulge their location or show them to anyone. After shrinking their son's head, Tukupi went to visit the parents of the slain boy. He asked them not to seek vengeance and began to sing to them: "I'm an anaconda man. If you come to search for me, I will transform into a huge snake and devour you. Let your spirits be at rest. I'm an anaconda man."

Tukupi kept singing, and I kept recording—many tales of warriors, of heads severed, of spirits mollified. Although they did not match my cultural proclivities, I nevertheless admired the honesty of what I was hearing. Since the beginning of time, men have been the keepers of death. Just as only women can give life, it's been the unique privilege of men to take it. But what of the modern industrial culture of killing and war? Take a sip of Coca-Cola, press a button, and one million people are incinerated. Where is the connection to the power of death? To its mysteries? To its meaning? At the very least, the Shuar way required direct cognition of death, a participation in its experience and meaning, a reconciliation with its effect on the psyche.

I asked Tukupi to describe the role of shaman and healer and how he had been trained. It was evident he took great pleasure in discussing this accomplishment in his life, even though it had to travel to me from Shuar to Spanish to English, Maria and John hurriedly trying to keep me in the loop of the conversation. I was amazed by his energy and potency despite his advanced age. Finally, as the evening unfolded, I turned to Tukupi and asked him, "You're acknowledged as a great warrior, feared and respected by all around you. When members of your community come to you for healing and relief from their suffering, you show compassion and mercy. So, Tukupi—warrior or healer: which is the hipper trip?"

He paused for a moment and his face lit up. He looked almost like a cherub. He peered straight into my eyes and with a grin, meant somehow to both frighten and disarm, he said, "I like them both."

▲

When it came time to leave, we couldn't get the plane started. No matter how much Gustavo tinkered and toyed, it didn't make a sound. John turned to me and said, "That's it, we're stuck here. There isn't even a radio, and there's certainly no power for the plane's radio. Someone in Miazal will just have to figure out that we haven't shown up and come look for us. Or we'll have to travel upriver by canoe for a week to get to a mission with a radio. I really don't want to do that." We all just looked at each other.

Interspersed between the cackling of the macaws, we heard what sounded like a small outboard motor. Sure enough, that's what it was. We could see downriver a canoe with a small—maybe five horse power—outboard motor. As it came closer, a white man materialized. He turned out to be the missionary we had heard about, one of the new breed who had committed himself to a life in the jungle and had lived among the Shuar for nearly two decades. As he pulled up to the bank and joined our small, befuddled party, he explained that he was from an Italian order, the same one that had loaned us the airplane, and that he had seen what was going on with us from his canoe on the river. In his mid-forties, he was amazingly well built, like a wrestler or weightlifter, obviously seasoned by and equipped for a life in the jungle.

He told us that he was collecting stories of the Shuar to be published by his order in Italy, emphasizing that rather than trying to simply convert the Shuar, they were now learning from them as well. He sized up our hopeless situation, then said, smiling, "Why don't we start up the plane?"

When we assured him that we had been working on it with no success, he countered, confidently yet modestly, "Hold on, I think I can do it." And he went off to the canoe. He returned with a rope and started winding it around the propeller shaft. I couldn't believe what I was seeing—I pulled out my Hi-8 camera and fortunately got it all on video. I'm sure no one would believe me otherwise.

After wrapping the rope around the shaft, he motioned to John, Juan Gabriel, the pilot, and Maria to grab hold and there they were, the five of them, pulling on the rope as though it were the starter of a lawn mower. Voila! The crankshaft turned and the propeller began spinning. The pilot yelled, "Quickly! Get in, get in!"—and hurriedly, without speaking, we jumped into the plane. We were off.

As we just barely cleared the canopy, John turned to me and said: "Are we really in this plane? I can't believe we're flying in this thing!"

I responded, "Not another word. Grace of God, we're on our way."

▲

As we rose from the canopy into the rain clouds all the images of the jungle disappeared into the light gray mist. We gathered our breath and calmed ourselves.

Flying now above the jungle, our senses saturated, it seemed our whole experience down below had been a dream, the kind only the magic of the jungle can create. We had been moving in that original dream, in a time before our great building up of the world.

John was actively engaged in environmental and cultural projects with the Shuar and it occurred to me that the tape recordings I had made on this trip could become the beginning of a much more significant project. I asked John if, on his next trip to Miazal, he would request his amikri Mariano to move among his elders with a tape recorder, taking down their stories and experiences while they were still there to tell them.

We wondered: How were the Shuar to survive with the influences of the world closing in on them from all sides? How was their spirit to be nurtured, and exalted?

John and I did not have the answers to these questions but we excitedly discussed what we might be able to learn—and share—if we could touch the spirit of the Shuar.

Ehud C. Sperling

1

Dreaming the World

A week before Christmas, a blizzard hit the Poconos region of Pennsylvania. I managed to land in Wilkes-Barre–Scranton just before the airport closed. I told myself that it was a good sign my luck was changing for the better, but my fluttering stomach did not seem mollified. I rented a car and drove through the swirling snow. Coming from Florida—and knowing I would return in a couple of days—I accepted the storm as a harbinger of Christmas. Another good omen, I hoped.

When I finally reached the power plant, I pulled up to the gate and rolled down my window partway. A sullen guard fought his way against the arctic air. He lifted the front of his ice-encrusted ski cap and peered inside the car. Recognizing me, he forced a smile, gave an abbreviated salute, and muttered something about a Merry Christmas. The gate swung open.

Bulldozers and trucks were scattered around the parking lot. Nothing moved, except the snow. The usual army of beat-up vans and cars was reduced to less than a dozen. The only sign that anything unusual was happening was the lights inside the plant. It was lit up like a Christmas tree.

I shut off the engine and sat there in silence. The mountain of black culm, a byproduct of coal considered noncombustible, loomed behind the plant. Would it burn? Would the fortune I had gambled pay off? I said a little prayer to Ayumpum, the Shuar god of lightning and fire, stepped outside, bowed to the black mountain, and fought my way against the icy wind toward the power plant.

Whirling snow followed me through the door as the men who clustered around the window to the boiler moved aside, opening a path to the place of honor. They shook my hand or patted me on the shoulder as I passed through them. Someone handed me a hardhat. I felt like I was wandering in a dream.

I heard the countdown: three, two, one. . . . The firebox erupted into flame.

Hardhats rained around me. The cheers were deafening. We were burning culm, a "waste." We had accomplished the impossible. Independent Power Systems was a success!

I had founded IPS in 1982 and been its president for nearly a decade. It was a dream come true: to build and own power plants that ran on alternative fuels and, in the process, to help clean up the environment instead of contributing to its destruction. But it was an industry that was not without its risks; nearly all other such companies had long since filed for bankruptcy, and their chief executives—my peers—were washed up, candidates for nervous breakdowns or worse. The Pennsylvania culm-burning power plant had been our big hope. Ironically, its success was the very thing that forced me out of the business. Once that firebox lit up in 1990, Ashland Oil Company made an offer we could not refuse.

Oil! The very industry I had railed against because of the destruction it was causing to the Amazon, that place where I had learned what college could not teach me. Oil, the industry whose terrible record of abuse, greed, and disregard for future generations had inspired me to develop a new model based on different values and environmentally sensitive technologies—here it was, ready to deal.

One of Ashland's subsidiaries had built our culm plant. The first time they had thrown the switch, nothing happened; the fuel refused to ignite. Ashland had been contractually bound to hire a German company, a competitor, to build a completely new boiler. It cost them a fortune (even by Ashland's standards) and punctured their pride. The chairman of the board wanted to recoup his losses and assuage his humbled spirit. The only way was to buy us out. He extorted us, threatening to tie us up in court long enough to force us into bankruptcy. He bribed us, making an offer that would provide me and my two partners with a very healthy return on our investments of time and capital. My partners were in it solely for the money. The

Ashland offer was their dream come true. We negotiated an even better deal and sold out.

On the morning after the closing, while I was in my old office packing up my personal belongings, I called Ehud Sperling. Founder and president of Inner Traditions International, Inc., he had published two of my books, visited the power plant that Ashland built for me, and become a very good friend. I trusted his judgment. "What do I do now?" I asked, explaining that at forty-five years of age I had no desire to retire.

"Listen to the advice you give in your books. Follow your heart. What do you want to do?"

I knew exactly but had avoided admitting it. "Change our culture," I said sheepishly. "Make the world a better place for Jessica." My daughter was eight at the time.

"What are you waiting for?"

"Where do I begin?"

He paused, but only briefly. "First, take me to the Amazon, to the Shuar, the people who changed your life back in the sixties and seventies. They were the source of your books—you'll find something there."

▲

We flew to Ecuador together and spent a couple of days traveling around the high Andes, marveling at the great volcanoes and visiting Quechua communities. Ehud kept talking about the Shuar. Each time, the mention of them hit me in the stomach like a lump of culm. I had not anticipated feeling this way, but there it was. I tried to convince him that the Quechua, descendents of the tribes that had been integrated into the Incan Empire, were more interesting.

"We came here to meet the Shuar," he reminded me. When I did nothing to arrange a visit, he started asking everyone we met—hotel managers, store clerks, tour operators, even taxi drivers—how to get to them. Eventually he learned the name of the one man who might take us deep into the heart of Shuar territory: Danny Koupermann. It was a name I knew well and one I had not wanted to hear.

Danny was the son of an old friend of mine, a man who had taken care of me when I had been a very sick Peace Corps volunteer in 1968. I had never mentioned him or my friend—who had died several years earlier—to Ehud.

"O.K., it's time you face whatever it is that's bothering you," Ehud said. He had sequestered me in a hotel room, promising not to let me leave until we discovered what was going on. I tried to deny there was a problem. He persisted (this tenacity is one of the reasons I count him among my best friends); he simply refused to let me off the hook.

Finally, my thoughts and feelings became too strong to hide even from myself. I could no longer hold back. I acknowledged—and had to explain— why I was terrified of revisiting the Shuar and the Ecuadorian rain forests, why I felt so . . . responsible. I told Ehud about the role I had played as a Peace Corps volunteer in the plan to colonize the entire Amazon Basin. The Peace Corps and other international development agencies had decided that the Amazon was to modern-day Ecuador what the North American plains of the nineteenth century were to the United States: a place that could accept its country's poor and at the same time become a breadbasket for the nation. The Ecuadorian government passed a land reform law modeled after the United States' Homestead Act. It encouraged landless peasants from the Andes to clear and farm the "vacant areas of the Amazon."

Unfortunately, rain forest soil is not like that of the plains. It is thin, nutrient poor, and washes away after the trees and their extensive root systems have been destroyed, leaving barren land that is unsuitable for farming, except on a very small scale, like that practiced by indigenous peoples, and for a minimal amount of time. Colonists worked desperately to clear the forests only to find that their farms were productive for a mere few years; after this time they had to move deeper into the jungle to begin the endless clearing all over again. Furthermore, the Amazon's "vacant areas" were only vacant by the standards of industrial cultures. To the Shuar they were traditional hunting grounds, the very foundation of their survival. Violent confrontations between colonists and Shuar turned into pitched battles. As a Peace Corps volunteer, I had felt caught in the middle and emotionally torn.

"But according to your writings you tried to warn your higher-ups about the futility of colonization—you even wrote a long memorandum about it," Ehud reminded me.

I agreed and for a moment felt relieved. Then I remembered the rest of my story. I described for him how, after leaving Ecuador and the Peace Corps in 1971, I had become an economic and management consultant to the World

Bank, United Nations, and other multinational organizations. "I returned to Ecuador and helped finance hydroelectric projects and build roads into the jungle. I did this in plenty of places in Central and South America, Asia, Africa, the Middle East." I didn't bother to mention that my feelings of guilt, coupled with the birth of my only child, Jessica, had been a major factor in my decision to leave the highly lucrative, secure field of consulting and enter the maelstrom of alternative energy.

He sighed and glanced out the hotel window at the skyscrapers of Quito and, beyond, at Pichincha, the active volcano whose massive peak shadows the city. "So you feel guilty? Full of remorse?" He looked at me and smiled. "Good. It's time to redeem yourself."

▲

Danny Koupermann had been eight years old when I last saw him. I remembered him as a small, pesky boy. Now he was a giant of a man, built like an NFL tackle, but with the soft eyes and sensitive smile of an angel—the type of man the Shuar could relate to. He barely remembered me, but he listened to us. When I repeated for him the story I had told Ehud, he shook his head and then said in a frank, pragmatic way, "You don't want to go back to the area you knew as a Peace Corps worker, John."

I glanced at Ehud. "Yes, I do."

"No." He chuckled. "A road runs through Limon now and down into Indanza, the area you knew as El Milagro. You don't want to see what's happened there."

"Because of colonization, because of what we did?"

He nodded. "The Shuar have changed during the last twenty years." He described how they had broken into two distinct groups. The majority remained in the land of their fathers, between the Andes and Cutucú Mountains, the region where I had lived that had been so severely affected by colonization, dams, and roads. These Shuar had adopted the white man's ways, accepting jobs as oil riggers, construction workers, housemaids, and prostitutes. A second, much smaller group had tried to maintain their traditional ways; they had migrated "beyond the Cutucú," over these mysterious mountains and deeper into the rain forests. Danny smiled. "These trans-Cutucú Shuar are the ones you want to visit."

"Can you help us do that?" Ehud asked.

"I can." He asked about our motives and, in the end, agreed to provide us with a small plane and introductions.

▲

Darkness comes to the equatorial rain forest like a jaguar pouncing on its prey: swiftly, silently, violently. From the open-walled Shuar longhouse, looking out over the swollen river, we witnessed a moment of brilliant magenta, the flash of purple, then—blackness. The cacophony of bird songs died as quickly as the sun, replaced immediately by the voices of night: the hoarse croak of frogs, the booming "whaaaank" of mating toads, and the occasional snorting of a wild boar foraging for food.

Seated on low wooden stools and a bench made from the side and bottom of a dugout canoe that had been the victim of the treacherous rapids down river, we were five men: an elder Shuar shaman, a young warrior, an old Catholic missionary who was half indigenous, Ehud Sperling, and me. Bats flew past our heads, in and out of the invisible nest they had built high in the leafy recesses of the intricately thatched roof.

Although the night had yet to turn chill, we sat before a fire. It was laid out exactly as I remembered Shuar fires of the past—three logs arranged on the ground like spokes of a wheel pointing toward the center, or hub, a design so simple that an infant can keep it burning just by pushing one of the logs further toward the center.

I found it difficult to believe I was truly here. It seemed so unreal that I'd lived in these forests, and yet it was hauntingly familiar, like one of those dreams that, when you awaken, you are certain you had before or acted out in another lifetime. It was indeed very similar to the place where I had been stationed in the late sixties—mountainous jungles, fast-flowing rivers, a land of macaws, gigantic trees, reptilian vines, and brilliant orchids.

Yet, flying in we had passed above that other region along the eastern slopes of the Andes, the one I had once called home. We had seen the difference. From our single-engine plane we had peered down at the devastated jungle, the roads built by North American oil companies, the shanty-town cities, the cattle ranches, and the mud farms of colonists. We had been witnesses to the onslaught of what we in our Northern schools, remote from the reality, call "development," or "civilization." Danny Koupermann had been right. It had changed. In twenty years it had been transformed from a verdant wilderness, hunting grounds of the Shuar, to a nightmare land of grotesque industrial skeletons, a parody of what we told the world we were creating in the sixties. As I watched the land pass beneath, I wanted to look away but couldn't—and knew I shouldn't.

Then we had crossed the Cutucú Mountains and the world returned to normalcy, or at least the normalcy I associated with the eastern Amazon. Miazal, located in a clearing along the Mangosiza River on the eastern slopes of the Cutucú, was like a mirror image of that other community, in another time, on the eastern slopes of the Andes.

"The Cutucú protected this area for centuries, since the time of Etsaa," the old shaman Chumpi* patiently explained. He sat beside the fire on a wooden stool carved to represent a turtle; despite his age—which no one knew—his back was as straight as a high-canopy tree. His face was deeply wrinkled and bore the dark blue tattoos that in former times told another man whether he was a member of a friendly clan or an enemy. The wrinkles and eyes were those of a person accustomed to smiling at the world. He wore his black hair as he always had, cropped in a straight line across his brow. He was naked except for a pair of faded red shorts, a concession to the modern world and a gift, I assumed, from the old missionary who sat across the fire from him.

"The Evias, giant white cannibals, let no one pass." He lifted his tumank, a bowed bamboo branch with a monkey's gut tied from one end to the other, a type of mouth harp traditional to Shuar shamans, and pointed in the direction of the mountains. "They lived on the peaks of the Cutucú and defended everything from here—" he swept the tumank toward where the sun had set, "to there, where the great river sea flows. That's what our grandparents used to say. The Shuar didn't venture into the mountains in those days, except when a warrior was initiated. But now, we who want to avoid the stink of the cities live here, on this side of the Cutucú. To get here we had to cross those mountains, risk the Evias. We took certain trails, those proven in the past to

*Also referred to as Kitiar in *The World Is As You Dream It* (Rochester, Vt.: Destiny Books, 1994).

be safe, but then it seems that anything is safer than living like those city people, in their dirty streets."

He paused to give me a piercing look, and then his eyes moved on to Ehud. "Anyone who wants to be Shuar comes here. Man or woman." His wrinkled face broke into a smile. "*Shuar* means *the people*. Only people live here." He laughed and leaned toward the fire. When he looked up again, his expression was serious. "Those who think that happiness comes from owning things, from clothes and money, aren't people; they stay back where so many of us used to live, in Macas, Sucua, Shell—along the Upano River or the Upper Pastaza. Those places smell like oil. The air is thick with farts from trucks." He touched the arm of the young man sitting next to him. "My nephew Shakaim Mariano went to the city, but he couldn't take it for long. Now he's back here, living like us, learning the ways of our fathers."

"I love the forests." Mariano nodded his head slowly. Although he was deeply muscled like a mature man, an athlete, his face gave away his youth. He peered into the fire. "Some of my friends have moved to what they call civilization. They say they like the money and the women." He glanced around, smiling sheepishly, as though embarrassed by the words he spoke. "They have to work very hard—at stupid jobs—and then they spend all their money on alcohol. Why would I want that life? I have everything here—my brothers, the woman I love, our family. I don't need alcohol; we've got plenty of chicha. I spend my days hunting, eating the best food, fishing, swimming, making love. . . ."

"As you dreamed it," Chumpi chortled. He stood and casually stirred the embers with a long stick. "That's how it happens. This everyday life is an illusion. Dreams make reality. We create the world."

"Shapeshifting," Ehud said.

Chumpi listened carefully as I translated. He laughed. "Soon I will shapeshift out of this human body into another form, the bat. It's my way. And you—." He looked at Mariano. "You'll be a great warrior, taking many heads."

Mariano nodded solemnly, as though he too had foreseen this. "Our dream."

"Mariano," Juan Arcos said, speaking for the first time since this conversation had begun, "You know you have a big job ahead of you." A deacon in the Catholic Church, only part indigenous but married to a Shuar woman,

Juan Arcos had brought the mission to Miazal some twenty-five years earlier. Because of him and his tiny school, Mariano was able to speak Spanish. Now, like Chumpi, Juan Arcos had earned the respect due an uwishin, one who knows, an elder who carries the torch of ancient wisdom. In appearance, the two men were opposites; Juan Arcos had no tattoos; was unshaven; and wore rubber boots, long pants, and a dirty shirt buttoned at the collar. Although his occasional smile was gentle and warm, his face was that of a man burdened with responsibilities, a shepherd ever vigilant for his flock. He looked at Mariano directly. "It will be up to you and your brothers to teach the next generation."

"I know," Mariano said solemnly. "I dream of following the footsteps of our great warriors."

"Jesus Christ was a warrior, too," Juan Arcos observed, crossing himself. "You must also teach the younger ones, your children and their friends, as he would."

Chumpi turned to face him. Each elder held the gaze of the other. The fire crackled. Outside, far in the distance, a jaguar screamed into the night. "I don't know much about Christ," Chumpi said at last. "I believe he was the shaman you say he was, but I never met him—not in the jungle or on vision quests while taking ayahuasca." He stood up and looked off into the dark forests. "But I've met the anaconda and the jaguar. I know the spirits who come when I call on them to heal the sick." He turned back to Juan Arcos. "You and I are from the same generation—although I am older than you."

"At least ten *ewi*!" Juan Arcos laughed, referring to the god of a palm that bears fruit once a year and is the primary measure of time for the Shuar.

Chumpi laughed with him. "Yes, I'm older and wiser than you. We are different, and we have our differences. You can read and talk about this shaman who lived long, long ago, in another place far from the Cutucú. I help people talk with their dead ancestors. I listen to you and respect your words and your books. But I know too that we must not forsake Tsunkqui; Nunqui; Ewi; Etsaa;* Ayumpum, who brings thunder, fire, and enlightenment; and all the others who have made the lives of our people beautiful."

*Tsunkqui, the first shaman, is the goddess of the waters; Nunqui is the goddess of the earth and of plants; Ewi is the god of the chonta palm and the seasons; and Etsaa is the sun.

"I agree, compadre. These traditions are important and must be preserved. The Shuar spirits stand alongside Jesus Christ."

I glanced at Ehud. It seemed an extraordinary statement for a deacon in the Catholic Church to have made. I could not imagine the pope approving this image of Jesus intermingling with Shuar deities. I decided not to mention it—for the time being. Instead, I simply said, "My people need this knowledge too," I looked directly at each of my four companions. "It's why we came here."

Chumpi, Juan, and Mariano looked at me directly in return. They appeared to study me as they might the footprint of an animal in the jungle. The world seemed deadly quiet, except for an occasional crackle in the fire.

Finally, Chumpi broke the silence. "I believe you. I know what has happened to the places where we used to live. I've visited Sucua and I've heard them talk about Quito. I know how awful it must be where you come from. No animals, no sacred plants or whispering rivers. Always remember that, though the world is as you dream it, sometimes we can't tell the difference between dreams and nightmares; we dream the nightmares into existence. That's what's happened in the Upano Valley and in your lands, my little gringo." He paused, sighed, and sat down. Lifting one end of the tumank to his lips, he plucked the single string and played.

The haunting tune transported me back to ayahuasca journeys I had taken two decades earlier. I remembered vowing that I would devote my life to great causes, to peace, to the environment. How I had failed!

When he finished, Chumpi looked me in the eye. "Your fate is to help your people shapeshift their nightmares into new dreams." He turned to Ehud. "And you. You are the tumank. You must spread the song among your people."

"You see?" Juan Arcos came and stood in front of us. "The words of a great man, one who knows. Go back and teach your people about the beauty of life, give them hope; I know that people in Quito and Guayaquil have lost hope. Padre Raul tells me it's even worse in Europe and the United States. But that can change."

"We can always change the dream. It's easy." The tumank returned to Chumpi's mouth. "Just change the tune." He played and the music of that simple instrument shifted me into another space. I felt the power of the forests. In my heart I knew that what seemed impossible could happen.

"Bring people here," Juan Arcos continued after the music had faded. He sat down on a stool beside Chumpi. "Not the ones who think they need to change us, but those who want to learn. Bring them here so they can feel the magic of our rivers and learn from uwishin, shamans like this old man beside me, about dreaming."

Talking with the Dead
in the Words of **Chumpi**

We know that men and women never die. Neither do the animals, insects, or plants. All of us simply shapeshift. We move back and forth all the time—a person becomes an anaconda, an anaconda transforms into a tree. It happens like that. We say that someone is dead when their spirit leaves the human body; they move on to another level, a different form.

The spirits of our ancestors are very wise, even more than the greatest of our living uwishin. After all, the uwishin is a person and therefore is restricted by the limitations we people have. The spirit-guide who comes in the form of an ancient one, our grandparent or great-grandparent, has passed through the vines that entangle the rest of us.

It may be that this ancestor has shapeshifted into a jaguar or an ayahuasca plant. Whatever the new form, this spirit is here to guide us. Our ancestors are teachers. We are well advised to listen to these ancient souls.

As a shaman, I often help people communicate with the dead. Really it's the natem [ayahuasca], which I prepare for them, that helps. It is up to the spirit of the plant and the arutam of the ancestors themselves—and the arutam of the patient. It takes courage to talk with the dead! [Laughter] Of course, I take the natem, too, and I can journey into their adventure, helping them find courage, assisting them in their conversations with the spirits.

But this is what I want to say: While I may sometimes help them, they must really do their work, face their fears, by themselves. The shaman can give a little shove—but that's all I can do, all I should do. Each one of the people I work with needs to go down into that dark hole alone, learning to communicate with the ancient ones, accepting their advice, and deciding what to do with it.

I know there are shamans who say they can accomplish all this for their people. There aren't many among the Shuar who do this—not that I've met. But one time a man came here who claimed he could talk with the dead for anyone who wished to hear them. He was with a group from some other country. He told his friends that those who were dead were standing near them; he described them in detail and repeated the words the dead said to him. I wasn't there, but I heard about it. I have to ask, "So what?" What's the point of someone else telling you what your grandmother looks like or the advice she offers? You must do the work. You alone. A good shaman might assist you, teach you a thing or two, help you overcome your fear—but soon he must let you go so that you can do your own talking and listening. Otherwise, he's not a good shaman; he simply takes your power and uses it to his advantage.

There are times when the shaman may intervene with a dead one who's causing problems. A spirit like this may be confused or not aware that he's shapeshifted. Spirits such as these could try to drag a living person with them, before his or her time. Then it may be necessary for a shaman to help. I had to help in this way during one of John's trips here—the grandmother of a young woman from across the ocean was terribly confused and wanted to take the poor girl with her. I had to fight the grandmother's spirit like an arutam warrior, a *kakaram* man, using all my powers. It was a battle, I can tell you—as I will another time.

In the old days—when I was young!—we buried kakaram men differently from the way we bury them today. These were the greatest of the warriors, men who had mountains of arutam built up over many lifetimes. When one of these men shapeshifted out of his human form, we propped him against the central pole in his longhouse and wove vines all around him, covering his body completely, as though he were inside a huge basket. That had to be done very quickly—the day of his death—before his strong spirit could get angry or escape. After that, we all fled that home. The kakaram man remained there, inside that basket, until the house decayed and fell back into the forest, reabsorbed to become one again with the trees and soil.

But before the house was reclaimed by the forest . . . oh, how then at night the young warriors came to possess that dead kakaram's arutam! Only the most stalwart of men dared it. Each warrior erected a little lean-to in the forest near that longhouse, crept inside the lean-to after dark, and waited. Each waited and waited, shaking, trembling with fear. This was the scariest adventure, the most fearsome challenge a warrior could undertake. Confronting a living enemy was nothing in comparison! The power of the spirit world is well known. In that twilight time, the pale dawn before transition to full day, awful things can happen. The kakaram man's spirit was restless, confused, often raging and murderous. This undertaking was not for the faint of heart, not for any man who feared death or could not look agony in the eye.

When each man received the word, he stole out of his lean-to. Alone. The word might come from Nase, the wind, or from the voice of another spirit-guide—if his heart was open and as tough as the hardest chonta wood, the man knew it was his time. He raced across the space separating his shelter from the longhouse of the dead kakaram, charged through the door, and rushed up to the body encased in its cocoon of vines. Then he stopped, faced the dead one, and asked for his blessing. He sought the favor of this old warrior, pleaded for mercy and help, and asked for a portion of the arutam that the kakaram had accumulated.

If the young man heard a favorable response, the raspy voice of the dead man's consent, a scream in the wind, he would thrust a hollow reed through the vines that protected the kakaram's body, plunge that reed deep into the heart, and, with all his strength, suck out the arutam. The old warrior—the man a priest would tell you was a corpse—would either release some of his arutam to this young man or kill him, strike him down right there on the spot!

Whew! What a time it was! After that, the young warriors who had received arutam from the dead kakaram had a special relationship with his spirit. They could go to that spirit any time they needed help. . . . You see, there was no intervention here, no shaman who talked to the dead for these warriors. Oh, no! They had to do it all themselves. It was the most grueling of tests; yet those who passed it were well rewarded. Not only did they gain huge amounts of arutam, they also obtained the guidance of the man who had passed over, shapeshifted out of his human form.

Today we don't do it that way so much—few men are kakaram enough for that! But we do talk with the ancestors, with our grandparents who have left their bodies. And that story I just told you about the old ways makes it very clear that each of us must take this path alone—well, alone but not alone, for the ancestors are there, beside us.

2

The Gender Dance:
Love, Sex, and Control

As time passed and my plans for bringing groups to Miazal solidified, Juan Gabriel Carrasco and I formed a partnership. He was an Ecuadorian—and a close friend of Danny's—who had attended Montana State University and was dedicated to building bridges between North and South. Juan Gabriel spoke fluent English, was a licensed Ecuadorian guide, had close relationships with the Shuar, and was an expert at equipping and leading people into remote areas. Our intent was to comply with the wishes expressed by Chumpi, Shakaim Mariano, and Juan Arcos, to bring people into Miazal in order to learn about Shuar traditions and their attitudes toward life. We agreed to use these trips as a vehicle to change the dream, inspiring people to create a more sustainable, earth-honoring world around us.

The entire Miazal community came to our assistance. The Arcos family offered us a lodge with room for sixteen guests. Although not the typical oval building with a hard-packed dirt floor, it was constructed in the traditional Shuar style of vertical palm slats. It consisted of eight little cabins, each with two beds and a wooden floor raised above the ground—a concession to the reality that visitors preferred to avoid close contact with snakes and reptiles. In the center of this complex was an open-walled round room with a thatched roof, a communal space where we could meet, talk, party, hold discussions and learning sessions with the uwishin, and participate in ayahuasca ceremonies.

Young Shuar men made themselves and their dugout canoes available to help our people carry their packs from the dirt airstrip that had been hacked out of the forests, down the Mangosiza River, and to the lodge. They also showed us how to shoot their blowguns, led us on treks to the waterfalls where they held initiation rituals and vision quests, guided us to other sacred sites, and passed along all kinds of information related to the birds and animals we encountered.

The women kept us supplied with *chicha,* their most important food, instructed us in the ways of the plants, and shared the stories they tell their children about the importance of respecting and integrating with all of nature. They traded beautiful bracelets and necklaces, which they made from seedpods, nuts, and shells, for flashlights and T-shirts. During one trip in particular, the women of our group admired the rich artistry of these necklaces and bracelets. Each was totally unique, and yet all were done with great care and style. Several people commented that they could easily be sold in upscale shops anywhere in the world.

Amalia Tuitza Chiazu, Juan Arco's Shuar wife, emphasized that all the jewelry was made sustainably. "These nuts and seed pods come from living trees," she said. "We cut nothing to make them, bring no harm to Nunqui."

Living near our compound and often helping to prepare our meals, Amalia became an important teacher to our groups. A spry woman in her seventies or eighties with long black hair that fell to her waist, it was impossible to tell her actual age, and neither she nor her family admitted to knowing it. She was an expert on plants and was greatly revered by her own eight children as well as the Shuar girls who often came to help in her gardens and study under her.

Sex and Beer

One afternoon, Amalia took a group of us into her house and invited us to sample the chicha produced by several different women. "We take great pride in it—," she explained, "—and so do our husbands! Each woman's chicha has its own qualities, its own special flavor. There are people who say you can tell a woman's character by her chicha—the sweet ones and the sour ones! I don't know about that for sure, but I think it carries some truth. I also know that a woman's chicha changes with her moods. Sometimes chicha is a woman's greatest asset—next to her abilities to . . ." She chuckled and gave us a flirtatious look, "produce children. You see, it comes from the yucca, from Nunqui, goddess of the soil, roots, and plants—and also from us, from our juices, our saliva. So, chicha is very sacred, part of Mother Earth and part of us—like our babies, created deep in our spirits and our bodies. Try it."

As the Shuar women passed the bowls, they were careful to turn their faces away from us, avoiding eye contact especially with the men in our group.

"If we look a man in the eye," Amalia said coyly, "that's our way of telling him we want to go off into the forest with him!" She explained that it was an old custom, and that although things were changing in this regard, eye contact between the sexes was still a very significant symbol. "No ambiguity," she said. "My sons and daughters have seen the world beyond the Cutucú. They tell me that there's a lot of confusion out there. Here communication is simpler. We know who wants to make love with us, and we're not shy about letting them know our desires." She stood up abruptly and announced that we were going to Shakaim Mariano's longhouse, adding, "You'll love the chicha there!"

We headed off along a thickly forested jungle trail. Although prior to flying in I had warned the group about the significance of eye contact, it had not really registered until now. As we walked through the forests, I kept catching bits of conversation about it. Our women, I knew, were wondering how they would be able to avoid looking into the eyes of Shuar men.

Amalia brought us to a stop beside a stream. "I want to tell you about the giant anaconda who lived here."

Before I could finish translating, Susan, a North American psychologist, interrupted. "First, could you please tell us more about this eye contact thing?" She turned to me. "John, you've known the Shuar for a long time. What's your take on it?"

"Let me ask you this," I began, "What do you think of the Shuar men's bodies?"

"Absolutely gorgeous," Susan responded.

"Then the good news is that you can examine them thoroughly. Everything except the eyes. You can look at their faces, too, just not directly into their eyes."

Many of the women exchanged suggestive glances. One of them asked where the eye contact tabu originated.

I paused, uncertain as to how much detail I wanted to provide. "You need to understand," I said, "that sexual customs are very different among cultures around the world. Traditionally, the Shuar haven't connected sex with fidelity and family loyalty the way we have. This isn't unusual among tribal peoples. They seem to recognize that sharing the ecstatic feelings of intimacy creates bonds and that the more people you do this with, the better for the community. The Abenakis of New Hampshire, where I come from, apparently felt this way, as did many native North Americans. Whenever a single man entered their village, a woman would join him. There was no jealousy or sense of guilt around it. On the contrary, it was viewed as an important sign of friendship and an opportunity for the tribe to gain new insights; anthropologists claim it was also an important vehicle for expanding the gene pool."

There was much murmuring and chuckling among the people in our group. I tried to summarize what they were saying for Amalia. She threw her head back and laughed. "My husband, don Juan Arcos, is a deacon in the Catholic Church. Imagine what he feels about these things!"

"Don Juan talked to us last night about some of the Shuar gods and goddesses," Robert, a New Jersey businessman, said. "I wondered about that at the time. How can he carry out his church duties, teach the story of Christ, and also sing the praises of Tsunkqui?"

"I've trained him well!" Amalia said, smiling.

"Don Juan is an amazing individual," I added. "Sometimes I suspect that he and Padre Raul, the Belgian missionary who's lived with the Shuar for nearly fifty years, have been converted by the Shuar more than the Shuar have been converted by them. Shuar philosophy and lifestyles are very appealing—joyous and pragmatic at the same time. But despite that, the mission here adheres to the dogma, insisting on clothes, monogamy, and monotheism."

"But monotheism doesn't fit with the Shuar belief in multiple gods," Robert insisted.

"I think don Juan sees those gods as part of a useful mythology, like Santa Claus—but," I could not suppress a chuckle, "I'm really not sure. Maybe he's been won over!"

At this, Amalia waved her hand as though dismissing a discussion that seemed irrelevant to her. "Now for that anaconda!" she said, as she turned to face the stream. She grinned with a certain relish as she began to relate the story of the female snake who had lived in the waters at our feet several years previously, when the stream had been much deeper, almost a river. "That girl was as long as two longhouses." She spread her arms out to the rocky banks. "And noisy!" She made a sound like the snorting of a pig. "Used to keep us awake all night. So what do you think we did about it?"

"Killed it?" Someone suggested.

She shook her head disapprovingly, her hands placed firmly against her hips. "Never! She was here first, before we arrived. This was her home and anacondas are sacred. . . . We put up with her and her noise."

"What makes anacondas sacred?"

Amalia's expression grew serious. "All things are sacred. We never kill anything unless we need to shapeshift it into our lives and ourselves into its life—through eating—or unless it threatens to kill our families." She glanced down the stream to its confluence with a larger river. "One day a flood came screaming down that river over there and washed away the logjam blocking its junction with the anaconda's river. The deep pool where the anaconda lived transformed itself into what you see here, a shallow stream. The anaconda went away. We haven't seen or heard her since!" She crossed herself, in good Catholic fashion. Then she led us across the stream and further into the jungle.

After walking for another half hour we came to a trail that headed up a hill to our left—to Mariano's home. Amalia cupped her hands to her mouth and let out a long "Ohweeee!" She motioned for the rest of us to be silent. As we stood there at the bottom of that hill, I thought back to my first trip into this area, the time when Chumpi, Juan Arcos, Mariano, Ehud, and I sat around a fire. Chumpi's prediction that Mariano would become a great warrior had come true. During the years since that first visit, as I continued to bring groups into Miazal, Mariano had gone to war, along with other Shuar warriors, defending the Ecuadorian borders against Peruvian soldiers in a dispute that traced its origins back to a time before Columbus.

In the distance, we heard what sounded like an echo of Amalia's yell. "The man is home," she said. "It's okay to go in. I'll leave you here. I need to check on some of the young ladies tending the yucca nursery."

After she left I explained to our group that you never approach a Shuar home without a warning yell and the type of echoed permission we just received. "If they hear or see an uninvited guest, they shoot first and ask questions later." Since the group was so interested in Shuar sexual mores I went on to describe how, in the days when polygamy was still widely practiced (up until the 1970s), when a man went hunting, his wives often invited young uninitiated warriors to their home so they could teach them the art of making love. Most men made a point of not returning until after their wives had responded to their "Ohweeee," since they had no desire to stumble upon them while they were teaching!

We crossed a clearing in the forest and were met by a small boy who motioned us toward Mariano's longhouse. It had recently been destroyed in an earthquake. We had to make our way around the ruins of the old house to the new one he was in the process of building.

Mariano greeted us with a broad smile and invited us into the small area that had been completed. Although there were not yet any walls, we were shaded from the afternoon sun by the newly thatched roof. As we settled in he told us about that fateful night. "Suddenly I was wide awake! The whole earth was shaking. I grabbed the babies, called to Maria, and we ran outside. Right behind us the place collapsed. A second later and we all would have been traveling in another world where you couldn't visit us—not today anyway!"

Maria began to pass the chicha. As it went around, people commented on how sweet it tasted. I translated for Maria and Mariano, adding in both languages, "Most everyone agrees that hers is the very best."

After a while, Mariano asked me if any of his visitors had questions. Nancy, a San Francisco pediatrician, wondered what their favorite activities were; she addressed the question to both Mariano and Maria. They looked at each other and giggled.

"We like everything we do," Mariano replied. "Or we wouldn't do it."

"But surely," Nancy persisted, "you must have some favorites." She looked at Maria. "If you had a choice, would you rather cook or tend the gardens?" Then she turned to Mariano. "Would you prefer to hunt or fish—or work on this magnificent house of yours?"

The young Shuar couple's eyes met, exchanging an unspoken feeling. Then Mariano looked at me. He had recently asked me to become his amikri and addressed me by the Spanish word that most closely reflects that relationship. "Compadre, of course our favorite thing is making love." Maria nodded her agreement as I translated.

The North Americans glanced around at each other, uncertain as to how to react to this innocent expression of something that would be tabu to admit to strangers in our culture. Undaunted, Mariano spoke again. As he did so his eyes, earnest and sincere, took them all in. "You people need to make love more often."

"How can you tell?" Robert asked.

"Looking at you, I can see it." There was a touch of humor in his voice then, but I knew by his demeanor that he was dead serious. "You'd look a lot happier and more relaxed if you made love more often!"

"You're absolutely right," Robert agreed. He leaned toward Mariano. "The trouble is our culture has a different view of that."

"Change it."

Reining in Their Men

We followed Mariano across the clearing that surrounded his home and through a patch of dense jungle. The staccato chatter of the cicadas was almost deafening. Huge green and blue butterflies swarmed around us. Suddenly we emerged into another clearing. In the middle of it sat a very large and ancient Shuar longhouse. Mariano ushered us inside. I had been here many times. This was the home of Rosa Shakai and Domingo Chumpi, Mariano's mother and father.

When our eyes had finished adjusting to the interior darkness, an old woman could be seen seated on a stool near a tablelike platform that traditionally has served the Shuar as a bed. She wore a light cotton dress. Mariano took me to her—his mother, Rosa. After she brushed the long dark hair away from her face, she warmly placed one worn, wrinkled hand on my cheek, and the other into my outstretched hand.

Mariano leaned over the bed. "Papa, my amikri is here."

A man's body slowly rose to a sitting position. He appeared frail and moved as though suffering from severe pain. Mariano said, for the benefit of the others in our group who were gathered in the longhouse, "I want to introduce you to my respected father, Domingo Chumpi."

The old man was nearly blind. I moved toward him to take his hands in greeting; he received mine and bent his face close as though he would kiss them. Instead, he studied them for a moment. Then he looked up at my face, smiled, and welcomed me. He spoke to his son in Shuar, his voice so soft I could barely hear it. Mariano talked with him quietly and at length, occasionally glancing over his shoulder at our group.

"So, you've brought white people here who want to learn from us?" Domingo's voice boomed across the room. I could see the surprise in our visitors' faces; his body belied the strength in his voice, which came from a man accustomed to commanding authority. "Good!" Slowly and deliberately, he swung his legs over the side of the bed. "What are we waiting for?"

One by one, the members of our group filed by Domingo, shaking his hand and Rosa's. As we were finishing and positioning ourselves on benches around the wall, Amalia entered the longhouse. She was followed by Maria, who carried in a bucket of chicha and the gourd for serving it.

When the formalities of drinking chicha were completed, Domingo asked what it was we had come to learn.

Susan immediately spoke up. "This morning we traded our old T-shirts and flashlights for your wonderful jewelry. Why were you willing to trade for old clothes of ours?"

Rosa answered her. "During my life, we Shuar have changed many of our habits—like wearing clothes and shoes. The missionaries brought us these things. Shuar never wore shoes or pants before, not in the days of my youth. We never went to school either. But we knew a great deal just the same; we understood things that are being forgotten today, about the forests, the plants and animals, and the worlds of the spirit beings.

"When my mother was a child, all her needs—including clothing—were met by the forest. Nunqui offered materials for the few clothes the people wore. The same was true when I was a child, but by the time I had my first baby, the Quechua traders were coming here from the Andes once or twice a year. They wanted jaguar skins, anacondas, macaws, and *tsantsas* (shrunken heads). We took their machetes and cotton cloth. The machete changed our lives, especially for the men. We women loved the cloth but used it sparingly. Who needed clothes? All the children ran around naked. My parents were often naked as well. We swam like that, lived like that. We were Shuar, people of the forests.

"No longer. My children and grandchildren must wear clothes, even shoes. If they refuse, they're not allowed at the mission. The school there is so important. I know that my children will be poor and considered as savages if they don't get the proper education. The priests insist on clothes, telling us that for a woman to show her breasts is a sin and that any girl who allows a man to see her bare body is a prostitute. How this has changed in one lifetime!

"When I was young, men expected their women to know all the plants. They also made sure that their wives could train the dogs and raise the children. We had to learn by working. We had no school. No books.

"We girls looked for men who were great hunters. They had to know the forests and the language of the tapir and the boar. In her days, my mother used to say, the men had to be experts in battle, able to defend their families from enemy clans. In mine, too, that was sometimes true—it all depended on where your home was. Of course, with the war now it's become that way again; we have to fear the Peruvians. Once more our men are warriors—they must be.

"But choosing a spouse today? If my son wants a good wife, he's got to know the things he learns in school: numbers, and reading, and the names of far-off lands. My daughter, too. The teachers tell them to forget about the old knowledge, that all of it's written in the books. 'Don't cram your heads with that stuff,' they advise. 'It's here,' they say, tapping on a book. Oh, my! They are the learned ones now, the teachers. . . . So young, but I suppose they know what's best. Still, I wonder.

"You asked about flashlights. My grandchildren can really use them. You see, if mission students live more than a two-hour hike from the school, they're allowed to stay overnight in a dorm. For my grandchildren, though, it's not that far. So every morning they march off through the jungle and back again at night—sometimes in the dark. They're trained from the time they're very young to find their way in the dark, but still, it scares me. There are snakes and maybe jaguars; along the river, caimans and anacondas are always lurking. You can see their beady eyes in the moonlight! A flashlight can save their lives.

"Of course, in my time we didn't wander outside after dark. We had no schools, so we stayed close to home. Or, if the family had to take a long journey to another region, perhaps, we stopped well before night and made a lean-to. I never saw a flashlight until I was an old grandmother." She broke out in hoarse laughter at this reference to herself, and we all joined in with her. One of the women in our group mentioned that she too was a grandmother. While she and Rosa exchanged a flurry of stories about their grandchildren, Mariano and I translated as fast as we could.

Then we all sat in silence. Outside, it had begun to rain. We were mesmerized by the sound of the downpour against the thatched roof. In the rain forest, the rain silences all other sounds. Even the animals, insects, and reptiles fall under its spell. Their voices, usually filling the forest with their racket and song, yield to the power of this element, or to the god of the lightning and thunder that accompanies most storms, the god known to the Shuar as Ayumpum, who is also the god of the vision quest, of ayahuasca and enlightenment

Finally Amalia's voice broke the silence. "A powerful moment," she said. "The jungle honors us." She glanced around the room. "If there are no more questions, I'd like to add something to what we just heard from Rosa Shakai." All eyes turned to her. "Long ago, when I was very young, barely walking, my mother started teaching me about the plants. Over the years I learned from all the women in my family—grandmothers, aunts, cousins, anyone who would share knowledge with me. I could journey into those plants—still can—to discover their secrets, share their powers. I know about the ones that are good for food, the ones for medicines. I know which are right for teas or soups to cure fevers and headaches or bad stomachs and which ones should be applied to the body as poultices.

"My daughters have also learned a great deal about the plants—and they've been to school, too—in Quito, Europe, and the United States. Yes! Can you believe it? I never even heard of the places where they've lived and studied. They tell me that in those places it is the juices of the plants, the chemicals, that interest the medical people. But here we know otherwise. It's the spirit of the plant that counts!

"We sing to the plants, and I teach the young women around here to do it according to the old traditions. You know that yucca [manioc] is special for us. We cook it, and we also make chicha from it. We Shuar couldn't live without that plant. Well, yucca grows beneath the ground, close to the goddess Nunqui. We have to dig out the tubers—the part we use in our foods.

Before starting to dig, we always sing to Nunqui, requesting her permission, thanking her, and asking if it's all right to draw upon the spirit of her baby. Only if she agrees do we proceed. Afterward, we bury the stems and leaves of the plant so it will be reborn.

"Yucca is like us, symbolic of all life, all the rejuvenation, the shapeshifts that occur around us every moment. It's a symbol of transformation—life, to death, to life, shapeshifting. It's important for us to understand the plants in this context, to honor and appreciate Nunqui and all the other spirits who help us. My children tell me people have forgotten this in Europe and North America and that they suffer as a result.

"We all suffer when anyone forgets. It is essential that we who show ourselves as people honor all the others around us, everything!

"Shuar women know these things about the plants—special things. While the men cut trees and hunt, we women talk with the plants. The men say they can speak the language of the animals, joining them in their very lives. Well, we women do it all the time with our plants.

"My children tell me that the world outside is very male—in North America and Europe, that men have cut so many trees and have built huge, tall houses that reach far above the tallest chonta tree, almost to the moon, it seems. We know that men will do this and will kill more animals than we need for meat, unless we women let them know when it's time to stop. It's the nature of men! I have to wonder why women in those places don't help their men to understand these things." Her eyes moved across our faces, lingering for a moment on each of the women. "Why don't you yell at your men? Tell them to stop!"

"How?" Bridget, a high school teacher from Massachusetts, asked. "What can we do to stop them from cutting more trees or going to war?"

Amalia glanced at Mariano and Maria; all three fought to keep from laughing. Amalia turned to Bridget and grinned, shaking her head. "Don't you know the answer to that?"

Bridget looked embarrassed. "Well, of course, I can think of one way."

Amalia looked sternly at her, but her voice was gentle. "Men are the same all over. My son, Peem, whom you may meet tomorrow, has been to your country. He speaks English and studied to be a pilot. Now he's returned. He tells me that men in your country are not so different!"

Mariano cleared his throat, leaned forward, smiling, and said as if sharing inside information, "We Shuar enjoy making love. As Maria and I said earlier, it's the thing we most like to do. . . . It takes two to make love!"

"All that is correct," Amalia continued. "But there are many ways that a woman can control a man." Then she asked me to tell the story of an exchange that had occurred several months earlier.

One of our groups had taken a long hike through the forest to have a traditional lunch at the home of a Shuar family. When we arrived, we entered the longhouse and saw the man of the house sitting on a wooden stool at the far end, his blowgun and several spears leaning against the wall nearby that separates the formal visitors' part of the longhouse, from the family area and the kitchen. He was wearing only a loincloth and his face was covered with red designs that traditionally are painted on before the arrival of guests. Each member of the group went to him and shook his hand while he remained seated. After that, we all sat along the inside walls, and Juan Gabriel and I proceeded to exchange news with him. While we were talking, half a dozen Shuar warriors entered; they had poled their canoes up the river and, after the meal, would ferry us back to Miazal. Each of them shook hands with the man of the house and then with each of us. They too sat along the walls, leaving him alone in the place of honor where he sat, ramrod straight.

According to custom, after this initial period of introductions and the sharing of news, the man calls to his wife, asking her to bring in the chicha. She carries out a large urn and a smaller bowl, usually carved from a gourd. With a flourish, she fills the bowl from the urn and hands it to her husband first (a sign that the guests have passed their friendship test and the chicha is free of poison!). After he has drunk his fill, she refills the bowl and proceeds to hand it to each of the guests.

On this particular afternoon, when the man called for the chicha, there was no response. He sat there in all his glory, alone at the head of the room, trying very hard not to look mortified. He called again. Still nothing, The Shuar warriors began to giggle; they made little effort to suppress their mirth at his humiliation.

Finally, a young girl appeared. She trotted up to her father and whispered something in his ear. He took a moment to consider and then nodded his head and spoke softly to her. She ran back into the kitchen.

Mariano, wearing a toucan headdress and a shacapa and carrying a spear made of chonta wood

Photo by Norma Asencio

John with a tumank and the great shaman Chumpi, dressed in his missionary-approved clothes, with a kitiar. Soon after this photo was taken, Chumpi shapeshifted into a bat and has never reappeared in human form.

Photo by Mary Tendall

Rosa Shakai, Mariano, Domingo, and Johnny outside Domingo's longhouse
Photo by Mary Tendall

Jessica, Winifred, and John visiting Mariano's family: Mariano; Johnny; Maria holding Jessica; Pascualina; and John's godson, Mariano. Mariano's new home is in the background.
Photo by Ehud Sperling

John with Yajanua Maria and her baby, Kisar (which means Sacred Place Where a Spring Is Born)
Photo by Eve Bruce

Yaanua Patricia, her Austrian husband, Helmut Gantner, and their children Nantar, the baby Yancua, and Amaru
Photo by Mary Tendall

Yaanua Patricia in traditional Shuar dress
Photo by Mary Tendall

Three generations: Juan Arcos, Amaru, and Peem
Photo by Mary Tendall

Yaanua Patricia, Amalia, Juan Arcos, and Peem. Juan Arcos is in traditional Shuar
dress for the first time in more than twenty-five years.
Photo by Mary Tendall

Marriage

During our trips, we frequently visited Mariano and his family. The North Americans were encouraged to ask questions, and these often led to detailed discussions among the Shuar themselves. Because it seemed to me that our groups were often focused on a desire to learn about Shuar sexual practices and other gender relationship issues, I asked Mariano if he could tape a discussion on this subject between himself, his father, Domingo, and his mother, Rosa Shakai. One night, when the three were seated together beside the fire in Domingo's longhouse, he did just this, taking his cue for the kinds of questions to pose from those he'd heard us ask, and often addressing the future listeners of this conversation as though we were gathered with them around the fire.

Mariano: Papa, please explain how a young man married in the days of your youth.

Domingo: It was not so different from how it is now, except it happened at a much younger age. The husband might have just passed puberty and the girl might be many years away from her own time of the moon—still a virgin, a child, really. This is how it was when I was younger than you, Mariano.

When a Shuar man was interested in getting married, he hiked through the forest to the area where the family of the young lady lived. He might have to travel by canoe and cross over mountains, but he would do whatever was necessary. He would try to kill animals on the way—birds or, if possible, a wild boar—to take as gifts to the family he was visiting.

Once there, he sat with the father, drank chicha, and related all the news of what had happened in his territory. Of course, the young man showed the older man great respect; he was humble and offered to help his future father-in-law with his work. He hunted tapirs and monkeys, the sweetest of the meats, for the family. He wandered deep into the woods and brought back the special palm fronds used to repair the roof; he even climbed high up there to the ridgepole to do the hardest work. He made himself useful, completing all the tasks the father would normally have to do.

Ernesto Chumpi, son of the great shaman, with a mock tsantsa. Real ones are not exhibited in public to avoid disturbing the dead spirit.
Photo by Mary Tendall

Shuar warriors in traditional dress
Photo by Mary Tendall

Peem on a bridge near Miazal

In less than a minute, his wife appeared, carrying the chicha. From then on everything went according to custom.

"So you see," Amalia said after I had finished, "That woman knew how to get her way, how to control her man."

"A negotiation," Robert observed. "He made some concession, and then she served the chicha."

"Such as agreeing not to cut more trees," Susan said, and Amalia nodded like a satisfied teacher whose students were comprehending the lesson.

"Interesting," Bridget mused, "that in our culture it's often the women who demand a bigger house and more furniture."

Amalia seemed shocked. "Why?"

"They think those things bring happiness."

"Ah, how sad," Amalia said, shaking her head. "Our people have never believed that material things bring happiness. Instead it seems that they always lead to problems. It's necessary to eat and shelter ourselves from the rain— that's all. Men hunt and cut trees because that's their way. It's up to us women to teach them restraint." She paused. "Because chicha is so important to us, and a source of pride for both women and men, women often use it to accomplish their goal." She asked me to give the group another example.

I thought back to earlier trips. One example came immediately to mind. Once again we were all seated around the inside of a Shuar longhouse, that of a different family from the one I had described in my first story. The chicha had made the rounds a couple of times. Because Shuar tradition forbids men to touch chicha with any part of their external body except their lips, when one of the warriors discovered a large beetle in the chicha, he called to his wife, pleading with her to remove it.

She peered into the bowl, shook her head, and saying, "I see nothing there," handed it back to him.

He stared at it with disgust—and humiliation. Very gently, he asked her to come to him. She took her time but did so. They exchanged a few whispered words. He nodded his agreement.

She lifted the bowl from his hands, peered into it, and in apparent horror exclaimed, "My poor husband! There's a bug in your chicha." She then made a great show of reaching in with a finger and flicking the offensive intruder onto the earthen floor.

Marriage

During our trips, we frequently visited Mariano and his family. The North Americans were encouraged to ask questions, and these often led to detailed discussions among the Shuar themselves. Because it seemed to me that our groups were often focused on a desire to learn about Shuar sexual practices and other gender relationship issues, I asked Mariano if he could tape a discussion on this subject between himself, his father, Domingo, and his mother, Rosa Shakai. One night, when the three were seated together beside the fire in Domingo's longhouse, he did just this, taking his cue for the kinds of questions to pose from those he'd heard us ask, and often addressing the future listeners of this conversation as though we were gathered with them around the fire.

Mariano: Papa, please explain how a young man married in the days of your youth.

Domingo: It was not so different from how it is now, except it happened at a much younger age. The husband might have just passed puberty and the girl might be many years away from her own time of the moon—still a virgin, a child, really. This is how it was when I was younger than you, Mariano.

When a Shuar man was interested in getting married, he hiked through the forest to the area where the family of the young lady lived. He might have to travel by canoe and cross over mountains, but he would do whatever was necessary. He would try to kill animals on the way—birds or, if possible, a wild boar—to take as gifts to the family he was visiting.

Once there, he sat with the father, drank chicha, and related all the news of what had happened in his territory. Of course, the young man showed the older man great respect; he was humble and offered to help his future father-in-law with his work. He hunted tapirs and monkeys, the sweetest of the meats, for the family. He wandered deep into the woods and brought back the special palm fronds used to repair the roof; he even climbed high up there to the ridgepole to do the hardest work. He made himself useful, completing all the tasks the father would normally have to do.

The man stayed for several days, spending most of his time talking with the father and doing his chores. Between the young couple there was some conversation; however, there was no lovemaking. Not yet. Even if the girl was old enough, they didn't express their affection physically. They had to be very careful about this during that courtship time. Everybody was watching to see whether they would make a mistake.

Then, after he had pleased his future father-in-law, the young man returned to his own house and asked his father to make the request for the young lady. His father agreed and one morning—very early, way before sunrise—headed off to the home of the intended. The two older men drank chicha together and recalled stories of their younger days, their romances, and headhunting raids. When the time seemed right, the young man's father spoke with great sincerity: "Will you give me your daughter to join my family as though she were my own? My son wishes to marry her."

The girl's father only looked around at first, acting confused, as though this was the first time he had ever considered that his daughter might leave him. (Domingo laughs.) Of course, he had been waiting for the boy's father to come, but would he show it? Oh, my, no! Finally her father responded with something like this: "If it's true that your son wishes to marry my daughter, she must not leave me yet. She doesn't know how to work; she doesn't know how to make chicha; she doesn't know how to train the hunting dogs. She's lacking in many things."

But the young man's father would not be deterred. He might reply: "Even so, my son loves your daughter. He's interested in getting married. For that reason I am making this request."

The girl's father might ponder for a few minutes—maybe even longer—taking his time, drinking more chicha. Then he would say: "I'll give you my daughter but she must not leave us until she knows all that she should. While my wives continue training her, your son will stay in my house, helping me and caring for my family, getting to know my daughter and all of us. I've already seen that he's a good man, and I'll take him in as my own son."

That was how the marriage request was made according to our custom.

Rosa: That's all correct, in general. But let me tell you how it happened between your father and me, the specifics of our courtship.

One day that young man—your father, Mariano!—came to my father asking if he could take me away, to marry me. After all the preliminaries—him working for our family, the things you just heard—my father agreed. But I did not! I wasn't ready for marriage. Domingo Chumpi was the first man in my life and I didn't love him—so I refused. He was persistent; he kept returning—and so did other men, but I wanted none of them. I was young—less than your wife's age [fourteen] when you married her—and all of the men were in their teens. It wasn't unusual in those days for a man to marry a very young girl—younger than I was—really more like the age a daughter of his might be.

My father was very upset with me. "Why are you like this?" he asked me. "You refuse those who ask for you. Why don't you get married? You're old enough."

I told my father, "Domingo Chumpi is already married. I want to be the first wife, not the second."

Then Domingo's wife left him, as Shuar women are allowed to do. You know, traditionally any woman can leave her man whenever she feels he no longer deserves her. She decided to leave, so I married him. I'd been a good daughter; I was a good wife. I made delicious chicha and tended my gardens, and I gave him healthy children—eight of them, and that was enough! I also trained the hunting dogs for him—and I gave him datura once. Only once! But I prepared the wild tobacco for him often. I myself took a lot of tobacco, but I seldom recalled the experience afterward because I would fall asleep. In the morning, though, my husband would say, "You dreamed well—you'll be happy."

Now he's way over eighty years old and I suppose I'm over seventy—so we've been together a very long time.

Mariano: So, that's it—how we arrange to get married. What my father and mother describe is still true today, except now we usually wait until the girl is older. Often the young man still lives with the family of his future bride and works for his future father-in-law. As for the Shuar having so many children—we have to, because we live deep in the jungle, far away from one another, where there's always the possibility of danger. We must have enough children so that our neighbors don't need to travel great distances to find spouses.

Sometimes in the past cousins used to marry because there were so few people living nearby, but that's not done much anymore—we're more civilized today and respectful of the bloodlines of our families. Another important difference between today and the past is that Shuar don't feel they have to marry only other Shuar; we intermarry with outsiders, too. Of course, this has brought about big changes.

Overall, quite a bit has changed over time. Today we have machetes, guns, saws, and matches for lighting fires. These have made an enormous difference. Imagine what it was like to chop down a tree before the machete, or the axe, or saw! Or to kill animals with only spears! Sometimes, our women tell us men that we cut down too many trees, that we overhunt the animals. This is partly because these new tools make it so much easier than it used to be. What's a man to do?

Yet, despite these changes, we've kept many of the customs of our ancestors—even though we don't always continue them in the same way. Nobody's told us to change our customs, and we always remember them and think about them. Some Shuar may have changed, but not so many—at least, not those of us who've moved beyond the Cutucú. Because our children and some older people have gone to school where teachers have told us how things are in the outside world, some of us have become curious, and we've tried some of these things. Mostly, though, we find that our own customs are better. Now that a number of us have learned different ways and even practiced some of them, we still have a desire to preserve our customs.

We know that the ancient traditions have been very valuable for the Shuar. After all, we've never been conquered, and we know how to maintain the balance that's necessary for long-term peace. Everyone should be willing to change; yet certain things are basic and necessary for the survival of all people.

Rosa: Change will always come, of course. But we Shuar excel at physical work. Our men cut trees, hunt animals, and kill enemies. Our women tend the gardens, train the dogs, and raise the children. How can it get any better than that? We have a special god who keeps all this in line, balancing the relationship between men and women—Jempe, whose animal spirit symbol is the hummingbird. Neither men nor women can live alone. Men need women for chicha—only women are allowed to make it, and of course, they need women for making love and children. On the other hand, women need men for providing meat and protection. All of us, including the forests, animals, and all that are not human, need Jempe to remind us that balance is everything. Jempe usually works his magic through us women. We listen to the hummingbird.

Jempe helps keep the family together. This living together as a unit hasn't changed, except that now there are communities built up around missions and airplane landing strips. In the past, the Shuar lived alone in the forests, as isolated family units, not in communities. This is still true, in part: I and my husband here live close to the homes of Mariano and his brothers and their families. But the mission and the airstrip are not far away. We live as a family unit, but we're not so isolated any more.

Mariano: Maybe it will help for me to tell my own story about my marriage. I married when I was nineteen years old. My wife, Maria, was nearly five years younger. She was very beautiful, and I knew that she'd be a wonderful mother for my children. It was simple: I fell in love with her. In order to marry her, I had to make arrangements with her father and mother. I was from Miazal, but she lived far away. I met her as a soldier when I went to war. Because she lived so far from my home, I couldn't send my father to make the request for her to join our family. So instead I walked alone through the jungle to ask her to be my wife. I had to return to the army soon, so I knew I wouldn't have time to do all the things I was supposed to do for her father to show him what a good son I would be and what a good husband and father I would be for his daughter and his grandchildren.

There was really only one way to handle it. When Maria's father and I sat beside the fire, drinking chicha, I told him what it's like to be a warrior these days. I told him about Arutam, the all-Shuar brigade, our marches through the jungle, our battles with the Peruvians. We talked about the tsantsa ceremony. Then I tried to describe my love for Maria, my desire to share his daughter. I was very nervous!—the way all men feel in those circumstances, I suppose. I told him I wanted more than anything to welcome her into my heart and my life.

After this, I also had to ask permission from Maria's mother. I thought I'd feel calm inside because I'd already told her father my feelings—but I was still very nervous! Finally, they agreed.

You know, today life is more complicated. Because we Shuar are Ecuadorian citizens, we have to abide by the laws. If we don't, our children won't be able to go to school. So after I received permission from her parents to marry Maria, I had to leave my home here and travel quite far, to the cities in the Upano and Pastaza Valleys, along that road that climbs the Andes to Quito. When I was there in those cities I had to walk on muddy streets, and take crowded buses, and breathe in diesel fumes going from one government office to another to arrange for the marriage documents. I first had to get Maria's *sédula* [citizen ID card]. My parents-in-law had to fill out all kinds of paperwork, including forms for the army. It was an incredible hassle! I sometimes had difficulty understanding why we had to have so many stamped papers—and why they had to be stamped in so many different offices! It was never that way before—marriage in the Shuar tradition requires no paperwork. In my father's time it was about love and family, not about the government and the church and all those men I'd never seen before and will never see again, sitting behind their desks and asking for my paperwork!

It seemed as though government officials required an explanation of why Maria and I wanted to be together. I guess love wasn't enough of a reason for them! It always has been for the Shuar—and still is. I wrote down, for the church and the government, that since I had plans to do business with my parents-in-law, I wanted to marry their daughter. What they wanted to hear, I suppose!

Finally, when we were finished with all the filing and we'd had all our papers stamped, we hurried to the market to celebrate with a feast. It was a beautiful time. But guess what? We *still* weren't done with the red tape! After the meal we boarded a bus and traveled to Sucua, taking that road that follows the Upano River, through what used to be beautiful forests and hunting lands of the Shuar. We had to visit another office to register one more time—this time with the Shuar Federation, not the government! At least it had something to do with other Shuar, people we know and who know us. Funny, isn't it? Even Shuar clans who've been our enemies in the past know who we are; they respect us. I would much rather file papers with them than with men who don't know me and never will.

Being at the Shuar Federation headquarters also gave us the opportunity to send messages to my family about all that had happened and ask them to join us. It was important for our two families to get together to discuss certain details. For instance, we had to decide on the best man and the bridesmaid.

Finally, though, it was time for the wedding! The best man was Urbano Juan and the bridesmaid was María Magdalena. They were witnesses to the civil marriage. It was Saturday. They brought beer, and afterward we all celebrated.

At three o'clock that same day I had to talk with the priest about the church wedding. He told me we would go to the center where the mission church is located so we could take courses about being married. My father never took any courses. In those days it was enough that two people loved each other and had learned from older people about the art of making love and of what it means to be a good husband or wife.

My family and my wife's family all came together for the church wedding. It was quite a ceremony—different from the ceremonies of our fathers and mothers but similar in that both families celebrated together; the feeling of unity was the same. After the wedding, we traveled to the house of my father-in-law, where we had a true fiesta—we drank lots of chicha, people stayed with us all night. This part of it was very Shuar, like in the old days. Both Maria and I were very, very happy.

Domingo: After a year my son came back to his own property, out here in the jungle, far away from the cities in the Upano Valley. Now he lives next door to me and his brothers, as it should be. The Shuar have always lived deep in the forests, apart from others. It's what we like best. Sometimes, though, we're surrounded by enemies. There are many dangers here—from poisonous snakes, boa constrictors, anacondas, jaguars, wild boars, to men who will kill us when given the chance. We have to stick together. Families must remain loyal and defend one another. So Mariano came back to his home with his wife, my daughter. Today, they have four children. They speak Shuar and learn Shuar ways—but in school they'll learn to speak Spanish and find out about things I can't begin to understand.

Mariano: We live the simple life of forest people. We're hunters who raise manioc and a few fruits and other plants. We don't have much money but have everything we need to live well. We're never hungry. My wife and children and I are happy. We want to follow the old Shuar traditions as much as possible, remember Shuar practices, the typical dances, the *anent* songs that make our dreams become realities, the songs of love, the songs of the shamans. Never a day goes by when we don't give thanks that we're Shuar and our home is here, in our forests.

Extramarital Relations

Domingo: One more thing about this man and woman business. Sometimes it happens that two people don't get along—it may take a year or more for them to find this out. When a wife isn't happy, she can simply leave her husband and return to her family. She can do this anytime. Later she'll find someone else. It's different for the man, however. He can't leave; he must continue to hunt for his wife and protect her from enemies. This isn't to say that he can do nothing about the situation. If he's deeply unhappy with her, he knows how to make life difficult for his wife, hoping she will leave him. Some men have even resorted to beating their wives.

Mariano: In the old days, if a couple didn't get along together, either because the man didn't work and hunt well, or because the woman found a better lover, they simply moved apart from each other. Today, some Shuar still do the same, although the priests tell us this is a sin.

Domingo: We used to say that men and women should know each other very well before deciding to have a family together!

Mariano: In order to know each other well, to have sex before marriage, a young man and woman will make arrangements to sneak off together into the jungle. This tryst might happen during that time when the young man is visiting the girl's family. But he has to be extremely cautious; he has to plan it so that they won't be seen by anyone, especially the girl's father or brothers. He puts his warrior's and hunter's skills to work—which, of course, impresses his future wife! She places her trust in him and listens to the plan he whispers to her. He sets a place and time for them to rendezvous. Then they creep through the forests and have their time together. For the Shuar this sort of liaison is always done in the heart of the jungle, where we can feel the presence of the spirits and listen to the songs of the night. My father says this was the way it was during his time, too.

Domingo: Once married, sometimes one woman is not enough to satisfy a man. Even though he may continue to love her, sooner or later he might be attracted to another young woman, fall in love with her, and court her. He may end up with two wives at the same time.

Rosa: And the woman may also take lovers. She might say, "I'm going to do the same as my husband." If she becomes interested in another man, she might take him as her lover just as her husband has done.

Domingo: In the old days, when there were headhunting wars and many more women then men, a man might have three or four wives, but when he had so many wives, he had to have a large house. Some of these women were the wives of his brothers, warriors killed in battle. The wives knew how to divide the house into spaces for all the children and how to take good care of the husband—each of them made their own chicha.

However, some women wanted to have their independence. As Rosa said, some took lovers of their own. Many of them especially liked the young men before they had been initiated as adults, while they were still virgins. The wives would teach these young men the art of making love.

Some husbands felt that it was okay if their wives made love with another man. They saw it as no different from their having other women and felt it was part of the passing of knowledge to another generation. Even so, they preferred not to know about it. As long as they didn't know, they didn't care; the wives could live as they pleased—as long as they were discreet. These men would do everything not to find out. Coming back from the hunt, they announced their arrival by shouting out to their wives when they approached their homes.

But just as some wives were jealous when a new woman entered their husband's life, some men were also jealous. They tried to catch a wife in the act. This type of man would use his prowess as a hunter to spy on her wherever she went—in the gardens or banana plantations. He would also follow the suspected lover. If he caught up with them while they were making love, he would grab his wife and hit her with the flat side of his spear or machete. Some men hit their wives until the women passed out. Then the two men would fight each other—often to the death.

However, if the lover tried to hide or sneak away while the husband was beating his wife, the man would pursue him, chasing him through the jungle and across rivers. If the lover managed to reach his family compound, the husband would stop. Even in his rage he wouldn't be foolish enough to enter the home of another family where he would be outnumbered by hostile warriors. Instead, he would return to his own longhouse and send word to other clan members and men who owed him their allegiance, inviting them to go to war with him. They would all assemble, drink chicha in a kind of prewar party, and then head out into the forests to see where they might find their enemy.

By now the lover of the wife had probably left his own family compound. So the husband's warriors would search the territory. Eventually they would find him. If he was alone, the husband might only beat him—or they might fight to the death. If the lover had his own friends with him, there might be a great battle. That's the way family feuds often started, blood rivalries that continued for many generations. Some of those feuds are still going on even now.

Mariano: What did that sort of husband do after killing the lover?

Domingo: He went home, collected his sacred tobacco and datura and his *tunduli* [drum], and headed for the waterfall. He might hike all day and all night, for several days, fasting the whole time. Arriving high up there in the mountains, he took tobacco to help him regain his strength and balance, his arutam.

For three or four days he flew with datura. And then, when he was able to walk, he would hike to the other waterfall. During the day, sitting beside the cascading water, he prepared ayahuasca. That night he would take the ayahuasca and then play the tunduli until dawn. When the spirits heard the sound of the drumming, they came to the man and gave him power and strength. He continued playing the tunduli, until the ayahuasca was gone—for three or four more days.

Then he returned home, where he found his wife. She did her best to appease him by being very nice to him. If his anger had passed, the couple might live as they had before, as long as he didn't catch her with her lover again. However, if he did find the two together making love, the husband would kill both the wife and the lover. That was their custom, and it still persists.

Mariano: A few of these things have changed since my father was my age. We younger Shuar have been to school, and we've listened to priests. Very few men have more than one wife, and we expect our wives to be more faithful than in the past. When a man interested in love comes to them, faithful wives don't accept him, so there are no problems. Some women threaten the man by saying they'll tell their husbands about his overtures.

There are women who aren't faithful, though. They seek out other men—even for just one night. This happens sometimes at parties and celebrations—and some men do the same. If a woman wants a man for the night, she sends him a signal by making eye contact during the dance, letting him know with her eyes that she wants to go into the forest with him.

Often it's the man who doesn't take care of his wife who has the problem. Really, he makes the problem himself. The root of the trouble is when a man doesn't protect and care for his wife.

Now for a few words about making love: Men and women don't make love at home, with their children nearby. Even those who aren't married go to the forest for lovemaking. It's the way it's always been done—men and women make love secretly, close to the earth, in Nunqui's bed. But most people don't make love every day. Men have always respected their wives, and since men don't always know when a woman wants to make love, they may wait a week or two. This practice has always been our custom.

Sexual Training

Domingo: I can tell you how I learned about sex and about the art of lovemaking with women. It was the same for all the men of my time.

When I was young, I didn't know how to enjoy sex with a woman. An older, married woman offered to teach me—as was our custom—but I resisted her. So she tried to seduce me. My parents had warned me to be careful in these matters—a man might end up getting killed over a woman. It was for this reason that I was afraid. When the woman offered to take me into the forest, I ran off. She chased me, and once she caught me, she took my penis in her hands. I discovered that making love wasn't so bad! Then I learned how to please her!

When I was older, I married a woman in Inirekis and taught her all I knew about lovemaking. In those days, the women taught the young virgin men and the men taught the younger virgin women. That woman from Inirekis and I had two children and another who died from influenza. Then she left me.

Mariano: As my father says, women sometimes hunted for a man, to seduce and teach. This happens even today. The reality is that women belong with men and men belong with women—that's why we exist as we do in this world, why we have wives and children. God made us this way. We Shuar men have learned how to love women. We know how to think with our heads and act according to our hearts. Sharing the ecstasy is essential. You can make love to create children or in a way so that children aren't the result.

Rosa: We women like to have many babies—children are our lives, children and plants. But we also know when it's right not to have another child and we understand the way to keep this from happening.

Mariano: Young girls are virgins, and in the old days, when they were betrothed at early ages, men had to treat them as daughters first. When a girl became an adult, the relationship changed. At that time, just as her husband was a man, she was a women. We all understand the difference between young virgins and adults.

I've learned about the customs we've discussed here—and about all of our legends and practices—from my parents. They are great teachers and wise elders who are happy to share their memories and recollections. This is our culture. We've lived like this for hundreds of years and more. Who knows how long? We still live this way.

The Origin of the Tabu of Incest
in the Words of **Peem**

How did the Shuar come to learn that sexual relationships between close relatives aren't good, that incest should be forbidden? It happened like this.

There once was a beautiful young woman who could have had just about any man she wanted. However, she developed a crush on her brother's handsome son. When her infatuation turned into sexual longing, she approached her nephew and encouraged him to creep into her bed late at night while the rest of the family was sound asleep. She knew she'd be discovered if she left the bed and went into the forest. She taught him about lovemaking and they enjoyed each other fully and ecstatically throughout that night—even though the woman's mother slept in the same bed!

The young man was determined to continue this relationship with his aunt. He used every ploy and shapeshifting device to keep their liaison secret. On bright, moonlit nights, he changed his expression turning his face into a sort of mask—so that no one could recognize him. During parties, he disguised himself as a stranger, danced with her all night long, and then left before daybreak.

The two were deeply in love with each other and the ecstasy of their adventures, so much so that it was terribly painful for them to be separated. They continued to make love, even during those times of the month when Nunqui gave the woman the greatest strength of fertility, running the risk that they might conceive a child.

Once, they danced with such intimacy and passion that they did not notice the rising sun. Suddenly they became aware that all their relatives were staring at them. The young man raced out of the longhouse and hid behind a thick tree. The woman's parents ran after him, but all they found was a caterpillar painted with beautiful, intricate stripes. It clung to the tree and rotated its head making a strange whining noise that sounded like "Tsu tsu!" which means "Hello, hello!"

Soon after that, the young woman knew that she was pregnant. No matter how tightly she bound her waist, she could not hide her condition from her mother. But she steadfastly refused to disclose the name of her lover.

Her mother fussed and fumed. "It's not right that he has taken you without offering me anything, not even a pile of firewood. You tell him that if he's a man, the least he can do is cut me a stack of wood!" She assumed that her daughter's lover was a warrior, that she'd been seduced by a brave man who would protect her and make a good father for the child.

That night the nephew arrived in the guise of a caterpillar. In his mouth he carried a twig which he deposited next to the fire. Back and forth he went, bringing in a small mountain of twigs. Then he shapeshifted back into a man and made love with his gorgeous aunt.

The next morning when the mother saw the tiny pile of twigs, she realized that the father of her future grandchild was not the warrior she had imagined, but rather that he was a man given to deception. She reprimanded her daughter and grew very angry.

The daughter refused to defend herself. She fled and hid in the nearby yucca gardens, remaining there until nightfall. In the next days, her belly grew very fat, yet the rest of her body diminished until she was no more than skin and bones. She became so thin and weak that she could barely make it to the gardens and back. One day she did not come home, even after darkness.

The mother took a torch from the fire and went looking for her daughter. Long before the light of day she found her lying beside a smoldering fire. Stepping closer, she was horrified to see that her daughter was dead. Then she discovered something else, something so hideous she could not believe her eyes. Millions of caterpillars were streaming from her daughter's corpse. She stood there, unable to move, watching as the caterpillars swarmed from that lifeless young body; like a river of tiny snakes they writhed together, flowed across the garden floor to the yucca plants, and began to devour them. The terrified old lady charged into the caterpillars with her torch, burning and slashing them into extinction.

Not long afterward, it was discovered that the nephew was also missing—and people began to fathom the true meaning of this mystery. They remembered the way the two lovers had exchanged glances and they understood the identity of the stranger who so frequently came to dance.

Ever since that time, the Shuar, though very loving and sensual people, have disapproved of sexual liaisons between close relatives. This is one of the reasons why the longhouse is divided into two sections, the *ekent* where the women spend most of their time and the *tankamash*, where the men entertain themselves and their guests.

3

A Brotherhood and Etsaa's Lesson

The hot water cascaded over me, threatening to scald every inch of my body. It was so hot that at times I felt sure my skin would erupt in flames. I tried to journey into it, to see it as the uwishin Chumpi had described it—"the fire from the center of Nunqui that penetrates your soul, the fire in your heart," to visualize the deep volcanic springs that were its source, to allow their cleansing energy to permeate me. I leaned forward, away from the cliff, and, shielding my eyes from the spray, peered up at the thermal waterfall that streamed down the sheer rock into the steaming pool at my feet.

Ehud called to me. "Over here!" His voice was barely audible above the thundering water. "It's heaven!"

I pulled myself away from the heat and steam and waded through the pool toward where he sat beneath the other waterfall, the opposite of mine, the one of freezing, glacial waters. As I moved through the pool, I felt the change in temperature. At first gradually, then rapidly, my legs transformed from burning torches to icicles; they sent the message of their shapeshift shivering up my body. I eased myself down next to him.

"The place where heaven and earth come together," he said. "Where the mountain glaciers marry Vulcan's fires."

We had hiked up to the waterfalls the night before. Although I had brought in many groups since we first visited Miazal three years earlier, this was only Ehud's second trip. Soon we would head back to the round room where we would meet Chumpi and Peem, Amalia and Juan Arco's son. We would talk, take tobacco, and in the evening share ayahuasca.

Now, as we moved back and forth between the heat and the cold through the tepid water in the middle of the pool, we talked about all that had ensued during the time since our first visit. The trips had become extremely successful in many ways. Not only did they meet the requirements stipulated during that earlier meeting with Chumpi, Juan Arcos, and Mariano; they also had inspired people from the United States, leading to the evolution of many events and programs. These included the creation of a new organization, which we named Dream Change Coalition (DCC).

DCC grew out of comments made by several of the shamans that the people who visited them needed a tribe back in the United States, a support system to help them continue the work they had begun while in the Amazon. The goals of DCC were—and are: (1) to change the "dream" of modern societies to a sustainable, earth-honoring one; (2) to conserve forests and other natural areas; and (3) to use indigenous wisdom to foster environmental, economic, and social balance. Although the trips provided the initial impetus, DCC quickly expanded to include workshops, educational materials, and POLE (Pollution Offset Lease for Earth), an innovative approach to offsetting pollution while conserving rain forests.

"So many transformations came from that first trip," Ehud observed as we began packing up our gear, preparing to return to Miazal.

"I'll say."

"Remember how reluctant you were to come out here?"

I smiled. "Yes, I do." I tried to envision for a moment what all our paths would have been like had I not made that decision to return to the Shuar—but I couldn't even imagine it.

Soon it was time to depart. We said our good-byes to the waterfalls and gave our thanks to Tsunkqui, goddess of the rivers. Then we began the long, difficult, and dangerous descent.

The river that is fed by the waterfalls has cut its way deep into the rocky cliffs of the Cutucú over the millennia, creating a steep canyon that is cluttered with moss-covered rocks, some as large as a Shuar longhouse and as slippery as winter ice on a New England pond. These fallen rocks have been torn from the face of the cliff by avalanches, an ever-present menace, and continually alter the course of the river so that no matter how often you trek to the falls, you never take exactly the same route. Knowing that the entire canyon is in constant flux, it is easy to perceive yourself as wandering through the playground of a spirit so gigantic that the human eye cannot perceive it.

At times the river swells to a height that makes it impossible to stay in the canyon. It can change from a relatively mild stream to a savage, deadly torrent in a matter of minutes; this may occur without warning, since the catalyst for the transformation may be a localized storm upstream that is invisible to those wending their way down the canyon, beneath the overhanging jungle. To escape such a deluge, the wary hiker must scramble to the top of the cliff and wait until the waters have passed, for the forests on either side of the canyon are virtually impenetrable to all except the most skilled Shuar hunters.

We knew we had passed the halfway point when we arrived at Evia's Flume, a particularly treacherous area. The canyon closed in, and the water was funneled through it as though one of the monstrous white cannibals reputed to inhabit the Cutucú were pushing it with a huge hand. The roar of the rapids was deafening. We had to climb up the slippery rock walls, hike through a sort of tunnel of brambled bushes clinging to the summit of the cliff, and then make our way down the other side. Along the river it was a distance of perhaps one hundred feet, but it took us nearly an hour to navigate it.

Once we were past this spot, the going was fairly easy. When we rounded a jumble of boulders deposited by a recent landslide, we saw Peem coming toward us.

Amikri Men

"I thought I'd find you," he said, greeting us warmly.

"Pretty good bet," I admitted. "Something wrong?"

"Good day for a walk, that's all. . . . Besides," he laughed, "I was afraid you gringos might get lost!" Peem was born in Miazal, but under the influence of his father, he had attended the university in Quito and then traveled to the United States to study for his pilot's license. He was an accomplished musician* who created songs that interwove the culture of

---

*Peem means "flute." Shuar names are not made permanent at birth but change over time to reflect personality and accomplishment. His second name, Tuntiak, signifies that he has the power of the rainbow that lives in the sacred waterfall.

his native people with those of the highland Quechua, Spanish Americans, and North Americans. He literally acted as a bridge between these four groups. He had recently taken on the job of organizing a project under DCC to help the Shuar retain and honor some of their old traditions, including dances and music, that were disappearing as a result of the mission and its school that had been introduced by his father.

The three of us walked together along the trail to Miazal. The conversation turned to the topic of the amikri. Ehud knew that Mariano had recently asked me to become his amikri and while we were at the waterfalls had asked me to explain this relationship.

"I told him what I know," I explained to Peem. "But I'd love to hear your take on it."

"First," Peem said, "it's important to understand the background. You can see how alone each family is in the jungle, far removed from neighbors." He stopped and spread his arms. "A man can walk for miles through dense forest and never see another person."

"Its incredible," Ehud agreed. "Isolated like nowhere else I've ever been, except, maybe, parts of the Australian outback—and that isn't jungle."

"Well, you know that since the time John lived here in the late 1960s, the Shuar population has increased from about seven thousand to around seventy thousand."

Ehud gave a low groan. "Yes, I've seen those statistics. Because of the laws against headhunting wars?"

"That and also because of vaccinations and reduced infant mortality rates."

"I often tell this to the groups," I added. "And I emphasize that such 'improvements' aren't necessarily welcomed by the Shuar."

"Correct. Except in a few remote places, like here, we can no longer live off the land as hunters and gatherers. It's become too crowded."

Ehud interjected. "And since the Shuar don't believe in death—but in shapeshifts into other forms— I assume that prolonging life isn't always the objective, as it seems to be in the United States."

"You're right. We believe that it's how you live each day—not how many days you live—that matters." Peem stopped walking again and froze. "Just be still a moment," he said quietly.

The three of us stood in silence, listening to the thunder of the rapids. The river had disappeared into the forest, but it was present through the roar it made as it swept down the canyon. Above us, the high canopy shut out the sun. Despite the fact that we were on the equator, at an altitude of less than one thousand feet, in a humid rain forest, it was not nearly as hot as it gets in the late afternoon of a summer day in Boston, New York, or Chicago. In fact, later that night the temperature would drop enough to force us to sleep under blankets. The great leafy umbrella over our heads protected us from the sun's ultraviolet rays while the absence of concrete and asphalt prevented the buildup of radiant heat.

"See how alone we are." Peem started to walk. "At least, there are no people. And yet, just three days ago on this same trail, a hunter spotted a large jaguar. All around us there are boars, tapirs, agouti, monkeys, hundreds of species of animals, birds, reptiles, and snakes. Some are dangerous." He paused. "But just feel it. The aloneness. Think how it was as recently as when you were in this area the first time, John, in the late 1960s. There were one tenth as many Shuar then as now. Think of it! How alone a family living here was, how cut off from others."

"Isn't that how the Shuar liked it?" Ehud asked.

Peem studied him. "Yes—it was our way. Many of us would still prefer it and want to return to that type of living. That's why we moved east of the Cutucú. We might like to forget about the schools and missions, the medicines and airplanes. But . . ." he brushed the air as though swatting a troublesome fly. "Well, anyway, I was talking about the amikri. I wanted you to get the picture, see what it was like in the old days—not so long ago actually, to have an appreciation for how it must have been, living alone in the deep jungle—no planes, no neighbors, just you and your family. And always the possibility of a sneak attack from an Achuar or a rival Shuar clan. The most dangerous threat to a man or woman here is not a snake or jaguar; it's another man, an enemy.

"So out of this situation grew the amikri. We translate this Shuar word into the Spanish *compadre*. We also use *amikchir*, which is even stronger, and *winia amikchir*, which means something like "very amikchir." In any case, all of these indicate an incredibly close relationship, the strongest bond possible between two men. And, of course, women have their own equivalent.

"According to Catholics, if you, John, become Mariano's compadre, then you are the godfather of his son. For the Catholics this is a special relationship. However, for the Shuar the amikri is even more. There is nothing at all like it in Spanish or English—no word and no concept that can compare. The whole amikri idea grew out of an ancient trading system." Again he stopped. He peered up into the canopy and spread his arms, as though gathering in the whole of the forest.

"Remembering that the Shuar lived isolated lives, each family in a small clearing with one or two longhouses and a few gardens, then for miles around nothing but dense jungle, the wildest forests on the planet, it's easy to understand the need for special relationships." His arms dropped to his sides; he took a few steps forward and motioned for us to follow. Within a few moments we had entered an open space where tall grasses grew. It was a pasture that had been cleared once at the urging of missionaries for an experiment raising a few cows brought in on a long, hard drive over the Cutucú Mountains. The sound of the river grew so faint as to be barely audible.

"You see, in the days of the headhunting wars, it was very dangerous for a man to travel outside his own territory—his traditional hunting grounds. Fierce warriors might be waiting in ambush. But trade has always been important to the Shuar. For example, we have salt near here—the reason this community is named Miazal [my salt]. The Achuar, who live further east, don't have any salt. They, however, make the finest blowguns. Even though the Achuar and the Shuar often fought each other in bloody wars, they have traded salt and blowguns for as long as anyone can recall." The trail wound across the field and back into the jungle. Through the branches, the river came into view again. It was slower here and much quieter, no longer squeezed between the great rock outcroppings of the canyon.

Peem had broken off talking as soon as the river appeared. Now he continued. "How could all this trading happen under such hostile circumstances so fraught with danger? Through the amikri. It works like this." We arrived at the river. Before crossing it, Peem knelt in the sand along the bank. With his finger he drew a large circle. "Call this Shuar Territory." He divided it into a matrix. "Each of these sections is the land some family claims as its hunting grounds." He pointed at a section at the outer edge of the circle, and marked it with a P. "If I live here, in P for 'Peem,' far to the east, my lands might border those of an Achuar." He wrote the word ACHUAR in the sand outside the circle next to P. He also drew several inverted V's outside the circle directly across from ACHUAR and labeled these ANDES.

The circle was now framed on the east by the Achuar and on the west by the Andes Mountains. "In that case, I would arrange to become his amikri. We would hold ceremonies and make vows of friendship. I could still fight against other Achuar, even his brothers, but not with him. I am sworn to protect him as he is sworn to protect me. So I could go safely into his territory with my salt and exchange it for his blowguns." He dragged his finger in the sand, through P and over to the next section, still in Shuar Territory, on the opposite side of P from the Achuar. "I would have another amikri on my western border, closer to the Andes, to civilization, though still deep in the jungle. This man might be Shuar, but, as you know, there were sometimes wars between one Shuar clan and another, so again the taking of oaths, the ceremonies, are important. I might trade my blowguns with this other amikri for machetes or axes."

We waded across the icy waters of the river, picking our way from stone to stone. Compared to what we had experienced earlier, this seemed very tame. I wondered how a river that was fed by the thermal waterfall could get so cold so quickly.

Peem led us up the muddy bank to the wide trail that would have us back in the round meeting room within ten minutes. "Now do you see why this amikri relationship is so important?" he asked.

"It made it possible to organize a pretty sophisticated network of commerce," Ehud said.

"Archeologists have found Amazonian artifacts in the Aztec ruins of Mexico," I added, "indicating that even before the Conquest, extensive trade occurred all up and down this hemisphere."

"And that custom still continues," Peem said. "It's not so much about trading salt, machetes, and blowguns any more as it is about friendship and helping one another, especially in times of crisis. Also, today we trade ideas and news. Through our amikris we learn what's going on in other parts, we hear news from the Andes about politics and relationships with Peru, and from further in the jungle we know about the activities of the oil companies and receive news from the front lines of our men who are fighting the Peruvians. Amikris from other countries, like you, John, tell us many things we never knew before. You also bring items in that we can't get here, books and paper for the schoolchildren, tape recorders, things like that."

"It's quite a responsibility," I said, "being an amikri."

"And an honor. When Mariano asks you to be his amikri, he's requesting something very important." Peem turned to Ehud. "Now, John must take it seriously. He must think about it. He should not accept unless he intends to honor it. He lives far away, in the United States, and should only do it if he knows he will come here often, if he will need Mariano's help and will have something to offer Mariano and his family in return."

As Peem was finishing, we found ourselves entering the round room. Chumpi was seated on one of the long benches. Beside him, steaming over the open fire, was a pot of ayahuasca.

Etsaa's Lesson for the Shuar

Chumpi had taken me on as his apprentice. My training began the first time I returned to Miazal after the initial trip with Ehud. Although he said nothing about his reasons, I knew he was following up on his prediction that my fate was to help shapeshift the nightmares of my people into new dreams. He told me simply that learning shamanism would help change my life.

Over the years he guided me on incredible ayahuasca journeys—ones that opened doors for him as well as me, providing us both with insights into the ways our two cultures were converging. He taught me to play the tumank, an instrument that is revered for its transformational music. He shared many of what he referred to as "ancient mysteries" with me and encouraged me to modify them so that North Americans could benefit from the wisdom they offered. In addition, he urged his nephew, Mariano, to invite me to be his amikri. He told me that Mariano represented a new generation of Shuar. "He's the bow of an old canoe, guiding us into unknown waters," he said of his nephew. "You and he share this in common, two canoes that are destined to journey together."

He had also been training Peem. Interestingly, Chumpi said nothing to me about this; I heard it only from Peem himself. However, when the two of them were together, it was apparent that they shared a special relationship.

Chumpi was deeply impressed with Peem's musical abilities and often urged him to play his flute.

He rose from the bench where he had been seated as Peem, Ehud, and I entered the round room, greeting us warmly, beaming like a child who's found a lost toy. He shook Peem's hand and laughed with him over some private joke they shared. Then he embraced me in a long hug, something he had learned from me (hugging is not a Shuar custom). When he turned to Ehud, it was obvious that he remembered him well. "You are the tumank," he exclaimed to Ehud. "The one who carries the tune to others."

He motioned us toward the bench. We sat down together and exchanged news in the customary fashion, and I played the tumank. After the formalities, Peem told Chumpi about our amikri discussions.

Chumpi nodded thoughtfully. "There's an ancient tale," he said, staring into the fire. The pot of ayahuasca was balanced at the apex of the three burning logs. "It will help you to understand. Long ago, when Etsaa still lived among the Shuar here on this level, on earth, the Evias came down out of the mountains. Until then they had kept to themselves in their caves in the highest peaks and had left the Shuar pretty much alone. Of course, no one ventured far into the Cutucú, for it was well known that any man who was foolish enough to do so would be eaten by those monster white cannibals.

"Why did they come down? No one knew. Perhaps, people thought, it was because they began to run out of food, or maybe they just developed an insatiable appetite for human beings. But come down they did—not just one, but a whole war party of them, loping through the forests, knocking down trees with their huge clubs, trampling gardens, burning longhouses, laying waste to everything in their path, eating people along the way. And once it happened, there was no stopping them!

"We were fierce, proud warriors. Our men fought valiantly against the Evias. Yet even our mightiest warriors, in the prime of manhood, filled with arutam, could do nothing against those monsters. Our spears were sticks jabbing at rock, shattering, our knives mere splinters, irritating the Evias, driving them deeper into a frenzy of bloodlust.

"It was as though those terrible giants possessed some magic, as though they were protected by dark forces. They tore our shields from our hands and played with them as boys play with the flat stones they skip across water. They devoured our women and children before our eyes, swallowing them whole, our poor loved ones shrieking for us to save them. Then they plucked us, the warriors, off the ground and ripped us apart, taking one piece at a time—an arm, a leg—dragging it out, torturing us, making those bravest of the brave, the kakaram men, writhe in pain, scream in agony, praying for the gods to shapeshift them quickly into the next life, a tree, an anaconda, a bird who could fly off to distant lands. . . . Oh, it was a most horrible time!"

He stood up and leaned over the fire to check on his pot of ayahuasca. From where I sat I could hear it boiling.

"You speak of it as though you were there," Ehud said.

Chumpi smiled at him but gave no response.

"The uwishin have lived many lives," Peem observed.

Chumpi returned to his seat. "Then Etsaa came to our rescue. He arrived by canoe. He was one of us, a Shuar from up river, but we saw in him a special quality. He was built like a warrior, yet his chest, his arms, and his legs were more muscled than most. He carried a spear and a shield with an image of the sun emblazoned on it. He had a look about him. . . . He announced that he had arrived on our shores to rid us of the Evias. 'I'm here,' he said, 'to show you new ways to live.' Those words made no sense to us at that time, but his presence gave us hope. Our women brought out chicha, and we celebrated.

"Etsaa had come with other men, warriors of his clan. But when he headed into the jungle, he told them to stay behind, and he alone crept through the trees to the terrible camp where the Evias slept, journeying by himself to the huge longhouse they had constructed that smelled of death, reeked with the stench of decaying meat, the flesh of our loved ones.

"None of us knows how he survived, only that he came back and told of the deal he had made. He told us he had promised those horrid monsters that he himself, by himself, would journey into the deepest jungle every morning before the light and with his blowgun and spear kill the most succulent animals—birds, monkeys, boars, and tapirs—and carry them on his shoulders to the Evias' camp. He would personally feed them the very best of the meats the forests had to offer. In exchange, they would not harm the rest of us. Those cannibals promised to abstain from eating human flesh.

"We could not believe our ears. It seemed too good to be true. Yet it also seemed an impossible commitment on the part of Etsaa. 'How,' we asked, 'can you do this? How can you feed so many of them, those huge, gigantic, insatiable men? How long can you keep this up?'

"It was then he told us the other part of the deal, the promise we would make him in return." Chumpi paused and stared out into the jungle beyond the round room.

"'I'll teach you,' Etsaa said, 'to use subterfuge, to set traps in the forest, and to poison their chicha. You Shuar have always prided yourselves on your courage, have always fought face to face. You have now learned that it is a futile strategy when you're confronted by a foe so much stronger than you. So I'll teach you another approach.' He held up a finger. 'Have you wondered,' he asked us, 'why the Evias were sent to plague you? Why the gods allowed this to happen?'

"We had wondered, of course, but even our wisest uwishin could not answer that question.

"'I'll tell you,' Etsaa said. 'Haven't you noticed how many animals you kill and how fast they are disappearing? Haven't you seen that you cut so many trees for your homes, your canoes, and fires, that the forests are growing thin?'

"What could we say? How could we respond to that? It was true; we had noticed it happening.

"'Hasn't it occurred to you that people have no real enemies, except other people?' Etsaa asked.

"This struck a chord, and someone among us shouted, 'What about the jaguar, the anaconda, the pit viper?'

"Etsaa gave that man a look that might have wilted a chonta bush. 'You call them enemies? How many of you have died from those animals? A few, yes, but enough to stop our populations from overflowing like a river after a deluge? No. For the truth is that men have no enemies besides other men. When you do not keep yourselves in balance, you are like the flooding river. You destroy everything in our path—you are no better than the Evias. You do to the animals and plants what the Evias are doing to you.'

"So, in that way, we learned our lesson. It became clear to us why the Evias had been sent down on us. We asked Etsaa what we had to do.

"'You must promise me that you will keep your populations in check,' he said sternly. 'Don't force the Evias to do this for you. If you are unable to accomplish this by natural means, then you must weed yourselves even as your women weed the gardens. You'll learn to shrink heads and you will make this a part of your life. You are warriors now, and you will use your prowess to protect these forests and all its inhabitants from those who look like Evias to the snakes, the agouti, the birds, and fish—you, the Shuar.'

"We looked around at each other. We saw the wisdom in his words. We understood that to all the plants and animals we were no different from the Evias and agreed to his conditions, remembering the teachings of the wise ones, that death is not an end, but a shapeshift into a new beginning. We promised him and ourselves that we would try to change our ways and that— as a last resort—we would kill off more of our kind in warfare.

"But that was not all. Etsaa had one more thing to say." Chumpi smiled at me. "About the amikri. He commanded us to form special partnerships with our neighbors. 'You will use these so you can trade things,' he said. 'The Achuar make the best blowguns. Let them make blowguns so you will not waste trees with your fumbling attempts. You have salt that is readily available in your mines. Trade it with the Achuar for their blowguns; in that way they can stop digging up land where there is no salt in their constant quest for it. Some of you are better at building houses, others at carving out canoes; do what you know best, and make arrangements to help each other, to preserve nature through efficiency. Form alliances, partnerships, create relationships that are stronger than those with your brothers or even between fathers and sons—a special brotherhood. Call these *amikri*.'

"You know the rest." Chumpi reached toward me indicating the tumank. I handed it to him, and he played a melody that was both sad and uplifting. Then he set it down on the bench beside him. "After we killed off the Evias using the tricks Etsaa had taught us, we immediately began creating the ceremonies necessary to form the amikri relationships. Etsaa returned to the deep forests and, blowing his magical breath out through his blowgun, restored life to all the animals he had killed. It was amazing how all those birds, monkeys, boars and tapirs came back to life, a beautiful shapeshift! But that was not all. Etsaa had yet to perform his greatest shapeshift." Chumpi stood up, walked to the edge of the round room, and peered under the eves of the thatched roof up toward the sky. "He said we no longer needed him on this level, the earth, that his time here was complete; in the future we could count on our amikris for all the help we might need. Then he rose up off the ground and, like a flash of lightning, ascended into the heavens, where he became," Chumpi pointed up, "the sun."

"Etsaa, the sun," Peem repeated. He looked from Ehud to me. "That's the Shuar name for sun, Etsaa."

"Next time you come back here," Chumpi said, "go talk to your future amikri and his father. Both are great warriors. They'll tell you about the old ways and the new—about war and balance."

Oneness and the Secret of Peace
in the Words of **Chumpi**

They call me Chumpi. Just that. No Spanish name. Some say it's because I was born before the Spanish arrived. Hah! Perhaps that's so. Some say it's due to my powers as a shaman, a shapeshifter, my arutam. Who knows? I am Chumpi.

Often when I take ayahuasca with one of my patients, we journey together. I can see what she needs, and I help to guide her—or my spirit helpers do, the anaconda, jaguar, bat, Tsunkqui, and the power of my arutam. Then the arutam enters her, she feels it in her heart, and I just go along; I learn as much as I can so that I may heal her and help in many ways. It's always an education for me! But she must do her own work; I am always careful not to get in the way.

This happened with John Perkins several times. I was training him, as I also trained Peem and my nephew, Mariano Chumpi. They're all powerful young men, and I've suggested to them that they work together, joining hearts to help Nunqui, Tsunkqui, and Ayumpum do their jobs, uniting people and nature—something that has come naturally to the Shuar, at least in the times before the mission, yet seems so difficult for the gringos.

You know, there's nothing more important than for people to shapeshift into nature. We must feel our hearts as the same hearts as those of the anaconda, the jaguar, the river, and the chonta tree. We must also feel our souls as the same, and our bodies as well. This is the spirit of oneness, part of the power of arutam.

I know that the priests teach otherwise, saying that humans are above all the others. How can this be? Is not Tsunkqui a woman, a human? Is she not a goddess, and also the water, the turtle, the caiman? Is not Tsunkqui sometimes, too, a man? And Nunqui—is she not the roots of the plants during the day and the trunk, branches, and leaves at night, as well as a woman? Ayumpum is the lightning, the condor, and also the ayahuasca vine—a man on earth, a god, and so much more! Etsaa—is he not a man, a great warrior, hunter, and teacher, and also the sun that warms us, our hearts and bodies, all day long?

What about the God of the priests? Is He not also the river and the mountain, the jaguar and the fish? Does He not love all these things—the stones, birds, and insects—as much as he loves me or the priests?

Was I not a tree? Will I not be one again? And the bat—I know that soon my human form will disappear when I shapeshift into a bat. Does this mean I have sunk lower, become something less than I am now? Of course not. We are one, the same. The priests see us as different, but that's an illusion. They tell us that our ayahuasca and datura remove us from reality. It's just the opposite. We see the reality in our oneness. That's the power of arutam—feeling the oneness. The priests hallucinate and in their confused state declare that man is above all others. We are not separate from these things in nature; we are them, and they are us.

That's why the Shuar had headhunting wars; it was a way to keep peace and fulfill our promise to Etsaa—peace for all of nature and among men, which is the same. You see, we know that men will keep creating babies and use up more of the land, kill more animals, and cut more trees—there's nothing to stop us. Only we people can take that responsibility. We can do it either by having fewer babies or by going to war. Our young men used to sing an initiation song about sacrificing themselves for this purpose. "I was born to die fighting, born to sacrifice myself for Nunqui, born to sacrifice myself for my children's children."

Look at us now! The Ecuadorian government and the missionaries have prohibited headhunting wars. A few still take heads but not the way we used to. And just see what's happened! Look at all the Shuar. Our population has spread like the strangler fig vine. We can no longer live off the land, from hunting and gathering alone. There are too many people!

The only wars we have are wars with Peru! And there's no peace for the plants and the animals. They suffer. They are us, we are them. So we suffer. The Shuar have become beggars, begging the mission for food and education, begging visitors for shirts and stupid wrist watches, begging . . . becoming like the others out there who have lost their way.

The only hope is for us to regain arutam, to feel our connection.

War, Arutam, and Balance

The next time I flew into Miazal I was accompanied by three beautiful and incredibly talented women.

Mary Tendall was a psychotherapist from Nevada City, California, who specialized in helping Vietnam veterans. Her highly successful approach to treating post-traumatic stress syndrome was based on techniques she learned from the Shuar. She had been a participant on one of the earliest trips Juan Gabriel and I led. Following several more visits to the Amazon, she too became a trip facilitator—and was one of the main sources of inspiration behind the creation of Dream Change Coalition. As a practicing therapist, she recognized the importance of establishing a network that could support people once the euphoria and excitement of the trips ended and they found themselves back in their homes, working at their same, familiar jobs.

Eve Bruce was a medical doctor, a board-certified general surgeon and plastic surgeon who directed a clinic near Baltimore. She had replaced a sick friend on a trip at the last moment for, as she said, "reasons I could not understand at the time." During the flight from Miami to Quito, she developed flu, which quickly evolved into a full-blown, debilitating sickness, complete with vomiting and a high fever. When a shaman cured her in a matter of minutes, it changed her life. She returned to Ecuador many times and was the first nonindigenous woman initiated into an elite circle of shamans. This led to her active involvement in combining indigenous and allopathic approaches to healing. Eve also created a Web site for DCC—www.dreamchange.org—that was cited by *Time* magazine as one of thirteen in the world that best represented the ideals of Earth Day.

Lyn Roberts-Herrick held a master's degree in Buddhist and Western psychology and had been a holistic healer for many years. She had attended and volunteered at several workshops when I requested that she accompany me on one of the trips. My previous assistant had dropped out unexpectedly, giving Lyn only ten days' notice before her first visit to the Shuar. Just as with Mary and Eve, it was a shapeshifting experience for her. Back at home in New Hampshire, she incorporated the shamanic work of the Shuar into her practice and created a job for herself within DCC, one part of which was editing and publishing *Dream Change Magazine*. She also cofacilitated workshops with me and expanded the trip concept to include visits to shamans in Siberia and intensive training programs with Quechua healers high in the Andes.

Mary, Eve, and Lyn shared a deep commitment to the DCC goals and had a profound respect for the Shuar and the wisdom they offer people from other cultures. They were extremely hardworking, dedicated to making things happen, and true agents of change. In addition, the lovely souls of all three women were reflected in their physical beauty.

Now the four of us were in the Amazon together. On the morning after our arrival, we headed off to my amikri's longhouse. I felt like a man in the company of three goddesses.

After responding to the customary shout from us, announcing our visit, Mariano greeted us at the top of the knoll near his home. He knew Mary, Eve, and Lyn well and was delighted to see us all together. Soon we were joined by Maria and Johnny. While they explained that Pascualina and my godson, Mariano, had left for the mission school at daybreak, they led us to the open door and motioned for us to enter.

As we stepped inside, we were greeted by a strange, ferocious, hissing sound. Lyn, who had entered first, stopped dead in her tracks, causing me to nearly crash into Mary. There, glaring up at us from the floor, was a caiman, a fierce relative of the crocodile. For an instant I assumed it was dead—then I remembered that sound! Its mouth opened wide, baring huge fangs, before it hissed again and lunged at Lyn.

She jumped aside; the caiman was jerked back by a rope around its neck that was tied to the central pole of the longhouse.

Eve moved to a spot where she could see something other than the fangs. "Just a baby," she cooed.

"Yes," Mariano agreed. "Only about four feet long. I caught it this morning down by the river, next to the trail you took to get here."

We all stepped in closer, curious, desiring a better look—but we were careful to stay beyond the radius of the tether.

"What will you do with it?" Mary asked.

"We'll keep it here a few days so that it can teach the children. That's the Shuar custom. Once the kids get to know it a little, I'll take it back and release it to the river."

Fascinated—and feeling relatively secure in Mariano's presence, we marveled at this beast that only hours before had roamed freely in the jungle near where we had recently walked. We talked about the other animals we had seen during previous trips—the wild boars, ocelots, tapirs, parrots, macaws, tortoises, and anacondas that the Shuar often raise as pets and instructors for their children.

Finally, we settled down into a small circle to share chicha with Mariano and Maria, the caiman, now quiet, in the center of our group. As we exchanged news, two of the hunting dogs rushed into the longhouse and charged the reptile, who quickly backed against the pole, opened his terrifying mouth, and hissed at the two hounds. The dogs froze until, after a moment of indecision, they glanced at each other and wagged their tales. Growling, they began to circle warily, searching for an opportunity to slip past those terrible incisors.

"They know better," Mariano assured us, laughing. Eventually the dogs gave up and headed back outdoors.

I told my amikri about my earlier conversation with Chumpi and my desire to hear what he and his father had to say about warfare—as it had been practiced by both generations. I assured him that Mary, Eve, and Lyn were also interested in hearing about kakaram men. Mariano responded in his usual, generous fashion; eager to be helpful, he offered to take us immediately to his father's home.

Domingo's First Battle

Domingo appeared less frail than the last time I had visited him, although his eyesight had not improved. He expressed great joy that I had brought three North American women to his home.

"My amikri brings lots of women here," Mariano observed to Domingo. "Including his wife, Winifred, and his daughter, Jessica."

Domingo laughed. "Mountains of arutam." He patted my knee. "Too bad my eyes are so poor. My son describes them to me, the gorgeous daughters of Tsunkqui." He paused and chuckled. "What a shame I'm so old; I might steal them away from you!"

Although Rosa Shakai was not at home, Maria had brought a pot of chicha. We drank two more rounds and completed the formalities of talking about all that had happened since my last visit. Then Mariano conveyed our desire to learn about Shuar warfare.

Domingo nodded his approval. "I can't think of a better subject." His son helped him to a bench near the fire while the rest of us sat on low stools. "In the days of my youth, we all knew how to fight in wars." Domingo's head moved around as he talked, like that of a man who could see each of us. "For us, it was just a game, like today when the young men play *futbol* [soccer] or volleyball—nothing more. Except the losers died. Cowards ran away, as they do in futbol, letting their opponent beat them to the ball."

"It was really like that?" Lyn asked. "A game?"

"War for the Shuar was a game, or maybe what you'd call a custom, a sort of test. Even today we march to war. Warriors are not cowards—they're ready for battle and know how to overcome all fear, fighting without hesitation. They understand how to kill. A warrior who is great becomes a famous man—the most famous, what we call kakaram. To be victorious in combat is easy for a warrior who has arutam, the power of the jaguar and the anaconda. He's brave because he has learned to shapeshift and kill his enemies."

"You speak from personal experience, don't you?" Mary asked, leaning toward the old man.

"Yes, I was such a warrior. I took part in fierce headhunting battles. Yet, for my first fight, I didn't go to war on my own, out of any personal grievance. I went because a man in my wife's sister's clan had been murdered. It was like being invited to a fiesta. No one can refuse such an invitation!"

He paused and said something quietly to his son. Mariano then asked, his voice showing the concern his father must have expressed to him, "Does he bore you?"

We all quickly assured Domingo that he didn't at all bore us. "Please go on," Eve pleaded.

After exchanging a few more words with Mariano, Domingo continued. "The man who recruited me was Shakar, father of the woman Atinya. He wanted to get revenge because they had killed his son, who had been buried in the earth secretly so that the family found no trace of him. Shakar declared war and asked us men to fight at his side. Our war party included Shakai, Viecha, Sharinkiat, and many others. In all, there were about twenty warriors, well armed, some with shotguns, three with rifles. Others carried our traditional weapons, those of our ancestors: spears, war lances and fighting staffs. And, of course, arutam."

Mary interjected, "Can you please tell us more about arutam? We hear so much about it."

He cocked his head in her direction. "Arutam is a powerful thing! Its spirit is carried in the teacher plants—natem, datura, and tobacco—and in the sacred waterfalls. We know that arutam was formed by our dead ancestors when they transformed themselves into the powerful animals. There are many arutams; they take the shape of the anaconda—we call the spirit of that great snake *panqui*—and the jaguar. The strength possessed by anacondas and jaguars creates arutam. One who has arutam, who shapeshifts into the anaconda or the jaguar, is also called panqui. Nobody can defeat him. All enemies fear him, unless they have more arutam than he does, even greater powers—those with the ability to shapeshift into something terribly powerful. The powers of the anaconda and the jaguar, those two warrior animals, are the strongest of all. For that reason, when men go to the waterfall and drink ayahuasca, they want to transform themselves into a jaguar or anaconda."

Domingo lowered his voice. "Now, arutam isn't any different for women than for men. It's a single thing. Both sexes can have it. When a woman possesses it—what beauty! What spirit! What magic she can work with men, children, plants, and animals! It is incredible to behold a woman or a man shapeshifting into an anaconda or jaguar, transforming right before your eyes. . . . What a sight! And to be transformed yourself—what an experience!" He paused and called for more chicha. When he had finished drinking, he handed the bowl to his daughter-in-law and indicated with a toss of his head that she should serve the rest of us. Lyn asked him whether arutam could be used in evil ways, to hurt other people.

"Arutam is a power that can be used for good or evil. Yes, it can hurt others. We live by its power. Without arutam we could not survive so long. Our enemies could kill us! People who live eighty or ninety years are the ones who have the powers of the jaguar or the anaconda and have presented themselves at the sacred waterfall when they took ayahuasca or tobacco. Those who live many years and have children and good luck possess arutam. They are the shapeshifters we all respect.

"Would any man go on a killing raid if he didn't posses arutam?" I asked.

Mariano replied, "He'd have to be crazy."

"Without arutam, the power of the forest, on his side, only a crazy man would attack an enemy," Domingo agreed. "In Shakar's revenge party we all had arutam. Every man was a kakaram man, although it's not our way for any of us to say so publicly."

Mariano stood and added, "To brag about such things is very dangerous. When a kakaram man boasts about his exploits, he loses arutam. Then he becomes vulnerable."

Domingo's blank eyes had followed the voice of his son as he spoke. Then he picked up when Mariano finished speaking, "He'll die in his next battle. We know that, and every one of us prepared ourselves for the fight without talking about such things. We did what we had been trained to do, readying ourselves, our minds and bodies and hearts, like our fathers and grandfathers had, doing everything necessary to enhance the powers of arutam."

Outside it had begun to rain. Mariano stood in the doorway, watching as the drops formed a puddle in the clearing beyond.

Domingo continued with his story. "We fasted, then hiked to the sacred waterfall. That rain I hear reminds me of the place. We stayed there for about a week without eating. We took tobacco and ayahuasca and drank a little chicha but ate no food. Oh, we felt the arutam! We saw it in the cascading water, sometimes a huge ball of light leaping out of the rainbow Tuntiak, who lives high up in the falls. We journeyed to the spirits and brought in the energies of the great animals, our ancestors, and *shakaim*, the soul of the forests. We exalted in our oneness. We felt the ecstasy of life!"

"Shakaim," I said, turning to my amikri, "your name."

Domingo nodded. "Yes. Even when he was young, his spirit was the forest." He paused. The rain pounded on the thatched roof over our heads, but not a drop leaked inside. "Finally we set out on the raid. We picked our way through the jungle, stealthily, over to the Rio Kusaimi. We found eight beached canoes and 'borrowed' them to continue down the river. Each canoe moved cautiously, like an anaconda slithering through the current—brave, determined, quiet. Then we approached the bend in the river where our enemy lived. What a morning! As the sun was rising, we landed the canoes, crept up the bank, and quietly surrounded the longhouse. Oh, how our hearts beat! We knew we had succeeded in taking them by surprise!"

"There's nothing to compare!" Mariano returned to the stool where he had been sitting.

"Some of our men rushed the main door and guarded it, then charged inside. Others raced in through the kitchen to try to prevent the enemy from escaping. The sunlight hadn't yet reached the house, and the fire had burned down to embers—it was as dark as midnight inside. Someone brandished a torch, casting an eerie, ghoulish light into the room.

"In the confusion that followed, the enemy managed to escape; they fled into another longhouse nearby, closer to the river, taking all their weapons except a rifle, which was left behind. The air was filled with battle cries and the screams of terrified women.

"Surrounding this second house the same way, we were finally rewarded. We killed two of that murderous family that early morning. Keen fought back valiantly but was the first to die. Pertsen was also killed. Juank fled, vanishing like a ghost into the jungle.

"Someone learned that a warrior named Tangamash was farther down river, trying to escape. Three or four of our warriors found him crouching in a canoe, hiding like an old woman. Waroosh shot him in the back, injuring but not killing him; he screamed for help, but our men seized him. Tangamash begged them, pleading for his life, explaining that he hadn't killed anyone.

Even so, he was a warrior, part of the enemy's camp. We shot him until he died.

"After killing the enemy, we didn't wait around. We hurried back to our families, jubilant, prepared to hold ceremonies. We celebrated our victories, feasted, drank our wives' chicha, and made ready to perform the tsantsa dance.

"So that was my first battle. In this way, I found that war kills anyone who does not have the power of arutam and protects those who do."

Headhunting, the Tsantsa, and Change

Rosa Shakai had entered the longhouse while Domingo was talking. Quietly she had passed the chicha. Now she sat down on the bench next to him and leaned close to the fire, trying to dry her wet clothes.

Eve asked if she could give her perspective on warfare while the fire did its job.

"I've always lived with it," Rosa said, matter-of-factly. "Just as my husband was a great warrior, so was my father, the man whose permission he had to seek in order to marry me. My father took the heads of many enemies."

"Would you be willing to tell us about how he shrunk them?" Lyn wanted to know.

"First, he made a cut up the back of the severed head and part way across the top." Rosa's hands moved over her own head to illustrate exactly where the cuts were made. "He took out the skull and meat and offered it to Tsunkqui, the river spirit. Then the shrinking process began. The mouth and all the other openings were sewn shut so the avenging spirit of the dead enemy couldn't escape and come back to harm us. After that he boiled it in a pot of water. Every night, as it got smaller, he filled it with hot rocks to continue the shrinking, and he molded it with a small stick so it would keep its shape. During the final stage of the process, he used hot sand, heated in the fire. The tsantsa, of course, is a sacred spirit. It must be kept clean and dry, away from any animals or worms that might damage it; it must always be treated with the utmost respect."

"Nowadays," Mariano interrupted, "we sometimes shrink the heads of slain animals."

"That's right," Rosa agreed. "We often shrink the head of the giant sloth and use it in the ceremony for initiating young men into adulthood. Before, it was always the head of a human enemy, but that's changing. Only certain people are allowed to attend the ceremony. There are special songs and dances—it starts very early in the morning, before the sunrise, and lasts several hours."

She shifted her position on the bench so that the heat of the fire could reach the back of her soaked dress. "Not so long ago a jaguar was threatening the people along the banks of the Tsuirim River—near where it flows into the Mangosiza, close to the home of Vicente Tuntuam." She turned to her son. "You remember that? Everyone shut their doors at night. During the day, the women were very frightened and took all kinds of precautions to protect their children. One day the women saw the jaguar eating something near one of the yucca fields.

"The shamans decided enough was enough. Something was wrong with this jaguar—it had been possessed by a spirit that needed to shapeshift. So the young warriors took the dogs and went after it—one of my own sons included!" She handed the chicha bowl to Mariano. "There were three dogs, all barking and furious. Finally they caught up with the jaguar and killed it with a gunshot.

"The tsantsa ceremony was performed and the jaguar's head was shrunk. We hold jaguars in great respect, but when one acts the way that one did, we know it's time for it to transform. Shrinking its head and showing it the proper respect and ceremony helps its soul move on."

"Because of these changes," Mariano said, returning the bowl to his mother, "such as shrinking animal heads instead of men's, some say the Shuar of today are cowards, but nothing could be further from the truth. Even though we've changed some of our practices, we're still valiant warriors. Shuar men still have arutam—time hasn't changed this. And the same holds true for our women. In the past, when a woman's husband was slain, the killer might choose to murder her as well. Shuar women have had to face death—they, too, know how to die—but they have always had arutam and still do."

"What happened," Lyn asked, "if you found a murdered man but had no idea who did it?"

For a long moment no one said a word. Outside, the rain continued. The sound of it striking the roof shut out all other noise. The puddle in the clearing had expanded and appeared to be dangerously close to the open doorway. Just as I was about to point this out, Domingo spoke. "When someone killed secretly, the survivors went to a shaman for advice. If the shaman couldn't discover who committed the killing, everyone left the matter alone and lived peacefully. Often, however, the ayahuasca exposed the truth to the shaman. Let's say a son was killed and the shaman determined the culprit. Well, then the father would ask other warriors to help him seek revenge. They would hunt down their enemy, surround him, and kill him with a lance or gun. There are many legends about revenge and war. People who had a great deal of power could kill ten or more enemies. Tukupi is a famous warrior who's still alive today. He killed more than thirty enemies.

"Now, as you might expect, the killer wouldn't remain at home waiting to be caught—he would try to escape. At night he might flee to the jungle or into the hills to save his life."

While Domingo accepted the chicha bowl from his wife and drank a long draft, Mary spoke directly to Rosa. "Can you please tell us more about the tsantsa ceremony?"

"We take only the head of the slain enemy. The warriors cut it from the body and carry it home. After they've returned to their families, the severed head is shrunk, making a tsantsa of the enemy we killed, and then a great ceremony is held.

"On the day of the ceremony, in the afternoon, we begin the feast. The old men and women come forward, followed by the married men and women, who eat together, face to face. When the unmarried young men receive food, they pass it to their mothers and sisters before they help themselves. This is a sign of respect and a symbol of the balance between nature that Jempe, the hummingbird god of balance, loves to witness.

"Then a woman and a man are designated as the ceremonial couple. The drums start to beat. The woman, wearing a *shacapa* [a belt decorated with beads and shells] around her waist holds onto the man who wears a similar shacapa around his shoulders and, jumping up and down, she dances forward with the man. They carry the shrunken head, the tsantsa, with two older uwishin guiding them. The woman and man dance between the two elders, and this is how they learn and are initiated into the tsantsa ceremony."

A Modern Warrior

After Rosa's explanation I mentioned that I had read an excerpt from one of the Spanish colonial chronicles describing a battle in the late 1500s in which the Shuar had killed 30,000 Spaniards in a single day.

"Yes," Mariano mused. "The Spaniards left us alone for over three hundred years after that day."

Eve then asked Mariano to describe his own experiences in war. "Though I know," she assured him, "that Shuar warriors don't like to brag about their exploits."

"They lose arutam when they do," Domingo grumbled. "It isn't so true for me," he was quick to add, "because it happened a very long time ago."

I held up the tape recorder. "For posterity," I smiled. "So that future generations of Shuar will have a record of your traditions."

Mariano looked at Eve. "I can tell you quite a bit without any problem." He moved his stool closer to the tape recorder. "Like my father, I've undergone trial by fire. My initiation as a warrior was very different from his, yet from another perspective it was the same. We both relied on the power of arutam, the spirits of our ancestors, and our oneness with nature." He stretched out his hands to the dying fire while his mother squatted next to one of the logs, pushed it forward, then blew on the embers. Flames shot up.

"When I turned eighteen years old I entered the army. I was in active training for one year, learning discipline and how to use modern weapons. I didn't have a chance to study the subjects that had been introduced to me in the mission school because the army emphasizes something else. While I was in the barracks, many of my ideas changed." He laughed in advance of his own understatement. "Army life is nothing like civilian life!

"After that training, I became a reservist. Our commanding officer told all of us who received military training that we have continuing obligations. Essentially, we're at the disposal of the army. A young man who doesn't serve his time both in intensive training and as a reservist isn't counted as an Ecuadorian citizen. That means he forfeits many rights not only for himself but also for his family and even the children who will be born to him in the future. A man who serves his country becomes a citizen—that's what we're told. Our blood demands that we defend our country. Our flag—the yellow, blue and red—tells us that we must defend our country as Ecuadorians."

Mariano continued matter-of-factly. "The Peruvians, our enemies on the southern border, have stolen territory from us. As Ecuadorians we must face up to them. We have to listen to the orders from our commandant and carry them out. If we don't obey his orders, we're nothing." He swept his arm through the air in front of him, as if erasing something invisible to the rest of us. Then he paused for a moment and looked directly at each of us. "So we're ready at any moment, even if we're at home; at his command, we must go to war.

"For any of us, war can mean death—but when we're called, we must do our duty. We have to leave our families and homes. Not only is it part of being a citizen, it's also the path of the Shuar, the same path as the one our forefathers followed. Not to go when called would be wrong. We're always prepared to leave here at a moment's notice, my brother and I. I have other friends living nearby who don't feel this way, though; they avoid going to battle." Mariano sat a little straighter. "But I'm not like them; I'm a warrior."

Domingo chuckled. "I agreed with my sons' decisions. They follow me in this regard. How can I expect less of them? I told Mariano, 'Go, my son. I'm proud that you're not a coward. Be brave! Cowardice is no good.'

Mariano continued. "For that reason, I said to my father: 'Datura, tobacco, and ayahuasca have given me courage and the power of arutam. That's why I think I won't die in war. I am a Shuar warrior.'" He added, almost tenderly, "My wife didn't want me to go because so many men don't return from war. . . . But we'd made our decision.

"My brother, Angel, and I trekked for days through the jungle, to battalion headquarters at Taisha. We presented ourselves at the command post, put on uniforms, and received our instructions, which we memorized carefully. Altogether we were eighty native Shuar. My other brother, Sergeant Chumpi, was waiting for us. He was my commandant. We were all like a team ready to fight, even after only a few days of preparation at the camp."

He paused to take another sip of chicha. When he glanced around at us, his face, flushed with the recollection of the camp's camaraderie, looked very young and innocent—yet I knew he had experienced a great deal.

Wiping the chicha from his lips with the back of his hand, he continued. "The colonel sent us a message saying that the other groups were ready for combat. When we arrived at the brigade, which we had named Arutam, they gave us our plans and equipment for combat, the weapons for the team to use in fighting. We were a powerful force, two thousand Shuar warriors determined to fight, to defend our homelands and families. We thought, who would want to face the Arutam brigade? What enemy could find the courage to challenge our powers, the spirit of the jungle, and our ancestors?

"We had nothing to eat—the army gave us only cigarettes. We'd heard that the regular soldiers, the Ecuadorians, complained about the lack of food. But we didn't. Our forefathers—my own father, as you've heard—took nothing but tobacco and ayahuasca before marching into war. We would do it the same way."

Domingo slapped the edge of the bench where he sat. "It's what gives us strength and courage, the power of arutam!"

"Though my experience was different from my father's—the army gave us cigarettes instead of liquid tobacco to sniff through our noses—the power was the same. We Shuar know that it's the spirit of the plant, not the form or chemicals, that brings power. It's the spirit and also the intent of the user. Our intent was pure. At night, when we were high from smoking tobacco without eating, we felt the spirit enter us. We were overcome with a desire to fight for our families and our country."

He stopped and tilted his head as though listening to the rain; then he pointed at the roof and smiled at Maria, who was sitting on a stool near the doorway.

"The following day, we woke to a deluge of rain—just like now, except we had no roof! But our orders were clear: we were to creep up into the mountains and position ourselves there. We did as we were told, but, lying there in the rain, we had no way to protect ourselves, no dry place for sleeping. We couldn't build shelters, so we shivered through the night, soaking wet and cold, all of us, my brothers and I—my father's sons, and all my other Shuar brothers. But, of course, we stuck it out and made it through the night.

"The next day, the rain stopped and the sun broke through—just in time for the head chief of the army to arrive in one of those huge helicopters, a Superpuma. His staff came in three other helicopters. Together they looked like gigantic wasps descending from the sky! We all lined up and stood before them.

"They told us to take our positions, and by late afternoon it was time to go to battle, the moment we'd all waited for. We were well equipped—each person carried four hundred rounds of ammunition and four grenades. Some of us lugged in other weapons, including the one we call *bomba atomica,* really a large grenade. But we still had no food."

I stole a look around the room. Everyone was riveted by Mariano's story. The three North American women, even his mother and father—all were intent upon his every word. It struck me that few of us ever hear such tales in this day and age. Wars are fought from desks or airplanes, or possibly from the inside of armored vehicles. How many modern soldiers go to war without food, slog their way through jungle downpours, or count on the spirit of a sacred plant to protect them?

Mariano went on to describe the battle. "The Peruvian army advanced. What a moment! We were vastly outnumbered but were determined to hold our positions. All night long they came at us, attacking with all they had—fierce, ferocious fighting; bombs exploding; rockets screaming over our heads. The sky sometimes lit up as bright as day. Then we charged them. We had to convince them of our superiority. We might have fewer men, but we were Shuar. Bravery and jungle skills count more than numbers. We raced down the mountain, shouting and shooting. . . ."

"Go on," Domingo urged, as though this were the first time he had heard his son's tale of heroism.

"The following morning at dawn we could see that the Peruvians had disappeared. Retreated. We'd overcome them." He let out a long sigh. "Although many of our bravest were lost."

"Amazing," Mary said.

Mariano only smiled at this, a smile that was almost boyish in its clear confidence. "We are Shuar. Arutam is our power. We defeated our enemies who threatened our lands, and we followed in the footsteps of our ancestors, all the warriors who came before us, the men who have become anacondas and jaguars, the great spirits who watch over us. That's all. Nothing so exceptional."

"I think it's an incredible story," Lyn said. "I'm so glad we have it down on tape."

"What happened after that?" Eve asked. "Was the war over?"

"Hardly. The Peruvians thought they'd win a quick victory. When they didn't, they sent up thousands of reinforcements. They're a big country compared to Ecuador. We continued to fight like that for three months—battle after battle, no rest, very little food. We sometimes felt that the army had forgotten us. We had three cans of rations a week for each man—when we were lucky! But we were determined to survive and to win."

"I have a Colombian friend," I told him, "who says that the Shuar have become the most famous fighters in Latin America."

Mariano laughed. "Possibly. At least it became well known all over that the Shuar were the bravest of all Ecuadorian soldiers. Even the Peruvians admitted how terrified they were to fight us, despite the fact that they always outnumbered us. We fought the hardest and were always at the front. Because we're accustomed to living in the jungle, we could stand the hardships of that kind of life better than any other soldiers. We know the forests—tracking, hiding, foraging, walking silently, invisibly. The power of arutam helped the Shuar."

He stood up and walked around the fire. Then he turned to me, a serious expression crossing his youthful features. "Yet, all of us—the Shuar—had to wonder why modern armies kill trees and animals. We understand about killing other warriors; that's the way it's always been—it's an expected part of battle. But the chemicals, the fire and defoliants . . . why use these? The land mines maim and kill animals and any innocents who wander by. Both the Peruvian and Ecuadorian armies—why do they fight this way? They say they're taught these things by the North American trainers. But why?"

I had to admit that I had no idea and that such practices bothered me and many others from my country a great deal. "Many of us don't approve of that kind of warfare," I tried to assure him. Mary, Eve, and Lyn all voiced their disapproval as well.

After a moment of silence, Mary decided to change the focus of the conversation. "When you returned here, how were you treated?" she asked.

At this Mariano's jubilance returned. "The community prepared a big fiesta for us. Everyone wanted to know how I was and what had happened. I told them that I was prohibited to speak about it—true kakaram men don't discuss these things. What happens in the army, you keep to yourself. Even with you here today, I've told only the general story, nothing about the men I killed or my most personal experiences."

Mariano returned to the bench and sat next to his father. "Like those of my family who went before me, I'm a warrior—and I'm still a reservist in the army, and proud. I'm ready for any emergency, prepared to serve the *patria* and the flag, the yellow, blue, and red. The red stands for the blood I'm prepared to shed so my children can live well and happily after I die."

"That's the attitude!" Domingo said, raising a closed fist. Then he turned to me. "If you want to learn more about war, you should find Tukupi and talk with him. He's as old as I am. In his lifetime he's become a legend, even among the Shuar—the greatest warrior."

"But to find him," Mariano cautioned, "you'll have to travel very far, even deeper into the jungle—all the way to the Forbidden Territory."

▲ ▲

A Tale of Nunqui
in the Words of **Rosa Shakai**

I was known as a Nunqui child. When I grew old enough to understand these things, my mother—Mariano's grandmother—told me so, explaining that from the time when I was just an infant I was obedient and quickly learned the things that girls should know, such as taking care of the garden plants, the domesticated birds and dogs, and preparing and giving datura to people who needed it. My father—Mariano's grandfather, who died before he had a chance to know my son—confirmed that I had quickly learned the ways of the Shuar women. That's why I was considered a Nunqui child. Nunqui is special to all people but most of all to us women.

Whenever we girls talked about our futures as mothers, I assured all my friends that I would have many boys. I knew it would happen because this is the balance: a Nunqui woman should offset her female arutam with many male children. And I did—seven boys! I was rewarded by the gods; none of the boys died. I also had one girl child.

Let me sing you a Nunqui song. (Rosa sings an anent, in which the sounds and emotions—not the words—carry the meaning.)

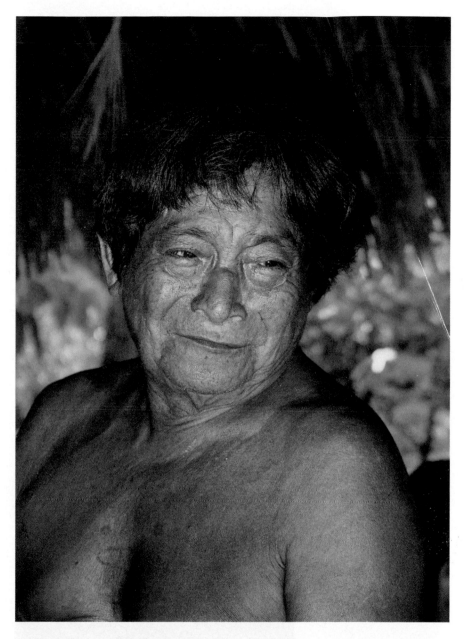

Tukupi, who killed thirty-three enemies—mostly Achuar—in hand-to-hand combat, is now a great healer for Shuar and Achuar alike. *Photo by John Perkins*

Ehud Sperling
videoing/recording
Tuntuam, who
is preparing
ayahuasca inside
his longhouse
Photo by John Perkins

Scraping the bark from
the ayahuasca vine prior
to cutting it up and
boiling it with other
"lover" plants
Photo by John Perkins

A typical Shuar fire.
As the logs burn they
are pushed in toward
the center.
Photo by Lyn Roberts-Herrick

Tuntuam preparing ayahuasca *(top)* and drinking chicha *(bottom)*
Photos by John Perkins

Daniel Wachapa preparing ayahuasca
Photo by Debi Christian

Lyn Roberts-Herrick with John
Photo by Sarah Severn

Mary Tendall with a three-year-old
peccary (wild boar)
Photo by Sylvia Wulf

Peem, John, Eve, Norma, and Juan Gabriel in the Miazal room where the Ayumpum
Foundation meets
Photo by John Hagen

A young Shuar girl. Her belt and jewelry
are ornamented entirely with seeds of
different kinds.
Photo by Mary Tendall

Ipupiara and Cleicha
Photo by Fritz Dent

Bosca Tuitza
Photo by John Perkins

Inside the Catholic church in Miazal. Above the tabernacle are a toucan headdress and a shacapa; at either side are spears, blowguns, typical Shuar baskets, and drawings of Nunqui with her baby. Arranged on the altar are turtle-shaped tsunkqui stools, named after the first shaman and goddess of the waters, who often rides a turtle.
Photo by Claudia Edwards

Shuar children in school clothes
Photo by Annie Pierson-Hill

Arutam Shuar: Members of the Miazal community dressed for a celebration. Men are holding blowguns and spears and are wearing shacapas around their shoulders, while the women wear them around their waists. At the time of this photo they had just completed recording a CD for Mary Tendall.
Photo by Mary Tendall

In case you didn't catch all the words, that was about love and ecstasy, thanking and praising the goddess Nunqui. We Shuar believe that ecstasy is the most important thing, that during our journey here as humans, we need to enjoy every minute. Ecstasy comes from that deep passion, the fire in your soul, from the sensation that we're one with all of nature. Make love often, and you will know what I mean!

In the old days, the Shuar did not eat as well as we do today. They didn't have the good food that we enjoy now. Instead they collected tender leaves and nuts in the forests. They ate only wild things, and they suffered as a result.

So this brings us to the story of Nunqui. As I said before, she is a special forest spirit, a good friend and helper to women. She lives below the ground all day long, working on the roots, nourishing and cuddling them as though they were her babies—which they are. Then at night she comes swirling up through the ground and dances in the forest. She weaves in and out among the plants, stroking them, breathing on them, singing to them, and tending to all the trunks, the bark, branches, and leaves. Oh, what love she gives them! What ecstasy!

One day, Nunqui was taking some time for herself. It was very early in the morning. Before returning to her duties underground, she went to a riverbank to eat a basket of nuts. Two Shuar women arrived at a place farther down the river. This was in the old days, before we knew about gardening, and these women were very hungry. When they stepped into the water to bathe, they spied nut shells floating along with the current. So they followed them to the source and found Nunqui on the shore, eating with great pleasure.

"Please," said one of the women, "can we eat some of your nuts?"

"I just finished," Nunqui replied. "They're all gone."

"But we're starving," moaned the other. "Don't you have anything for us?"

Nunqui pointed to a small child sleeping beneath a nearby tree. "I have this baby," she said, smiling sweetly. "She's very special.

Whatever she asks for, she receives. I'll let you take her. She can teach you things that will change your lives."

The two women were not sure what Nunqui meant, but they were grateful for this gift because children are always precious to the Shuar. They accepted the baby and took her with them back to their home in the forest.

Later that afternoon, the first thing the child asked for was a special drink that she referred to as chicha. Immediately a bowl of it arrived. The women had never seen or tasted anything like it before—so sweet and intoxicating! They were delighted. They shared the chicha that night with their husbands. Everyone agreed that it was the best drink they had ever had and that it also seemed to be a nutritious food. During the night, the baby came to the women in a dream and taught them how to make this delicious beer from the yucca plant.

The next day, the women asked Nunqui's baby what else she might offer them. A leaf appeared, wrapped around something that smelled wonderful. When they opened this bundle, they discovered wild boar meat. It was delicious. They shared it with their families, and everyone was extremely impressed. They'd never known that such delicacies existed! That night, Nunqui's daughter reappeared in dreams to both men and women, showing the men how to hunt the boar and the women the ways to cook it and even preserve it through smoking.

Over the next few days the baby introduced the Shuar to many other types of incredible foods: fish, an assortment of meats, and the multitude of fruits and vegetables that the Shuar now, today, have become so accustomed to eating.

Then the Shuar did something unforgivable. Forgetting the poverty of their previous lives, they neglected to give thanks to Nunqui and her baby. Lacking gratitude and balance, they became gluttonous. They began to cut too many trees so they could grow outrageous amounts of yucca and other fruits and vegetables. They killed many more animals than their diets required.

One day they were so preoccupied and so taken with themselves that they went off into the fields and forests and left the baby behind, completely alone and unattended. Nunqui, of course, was watching over the little one. She'd been watching all along and was both terribly disappointed in the Shuar and furious at their lack of gratitude.

When the people returned, the baby had disappeared. They were horrified. Frantically, they searched everywhere for her, but she was never to be seen again. The Shuar were left with the foods that the baby had brought to them—which are the same ones we eat today.

This experience taught our ancestors a lesson that they never forgot, one they passed on to their children, and to their children's children, and one we still, to this day, remember. It's why we women sing to the plants before we harvest them. We always give thanks to Nunqui and to her baby. We express our gratitude to the plants themselves, to the animals, and to the earth for all the blessings we receive. We women try very hard to maintain balance. We want to make sure that we cut no more trees than is absolutely necessary, that we kill no animals unless the meat is essential and every bone and feather will be used, and that every plant we take is replaced with a new seedling. Nunqui has taught us so much, and now maybe it's time to share her wisdom with the outside world.

"We Don't Die—
We Just Become Something Else"

When I returned to the United States, I called Ehud and told him about the discussions with Mariano and his parents.

"I'd like to meet this Tukupi." From the sound of his voice over the phone, I knew that he could barely contain his excitement. "You say he's in his nineties? Can you imagine the stories a man like that can tell? What a great opportunity—let's go!"

Ehud had taken an active interest in the Shuar and DCC. What began as the professional curiosity of a publisher for the subject of some of his books had turned into something more personal. He saw that the Shuar and the neighboring Achuar had an important message for the rest of the world. He offered his wholehearted support for my work and suggested that we organize another trip—one that would include a visit to the infamous Tukupi and some of the Achuar families who had suffered from his prowess as a warrior. Tukupi lived in the Forbidden Territory, so named because it was unmapped and unexplored, and because of its bloody history.

The Achuar—whose name, I had been told, derives from *achu* (a palm that thrives in the swampy lowlands to the east of the Cutucú) and *shuar,* designating the clans who live in that region—were an interesting dichotomy. The language and mythologies of the Achuar were similar to those of the Shuar, and many anthropologists—most of whom had never visited the

Achuar—classified them as a subgroup of the Shuar; yet they were a proudly independent people. In total their population was estimated to be about one-twentieth that of the Shuar; however, such numbers are deceiving, since in the Forbidden Territory, and in fact in all the lands east of the Cutucú, there were possibly as many Achuar as Shuar. Intermarriage sometimes made it difficult to distinguish between the two.

I promised Ehud that I would try to arrange for him, Juan Gabriel, and myself to visit Tukupi as well as the Achuar after the guests from my next trip departed Miazal and headed back to their homes. It seemed to be the ideal opportunity, since we already would be well equipped for the jungle and have a plane at our disposal. In addition, we would be relatively close to the areas where we wished to go.

Dream on It

Several months after Mary, Eve, Lyn, and I had talked about warfare with Mariano and his parents, a Dream Change group of twelve North Americans, two South Africans, and two Europeans flew out of Miazal. Juan Gabriel and I remained behind to spend a few days with our Shuar friends before setting off with Ehud on a three-week adventure that would take us deep into the jungle, into areas where no white men, except a few missionaries, had ventured.

"Tukupi has killed more enemies that any other living Shuar," Yajanua Maria Arcos Tuitza said, as we sat with her and her parents, finishing a meal of boiled yucca and freshly caught, steamed river bass. "Many of his victims were Achuar."

"I believe he's killed about thirty-five," Yajanua's father, Juan Arcos, agreed, "in hand-to-hand, man-on-man combat. Probably more if you count those he killed during the big raids in the old days, when a brigade of hundreds of Shuar took the warpath against their enemies." He smiled. "He lives near the border with the Achuar. Until just a few years ago, they were a constant menace, attacking our people in the forests, on the rivers, and in our homes. Tukupi was a great hero."

"You'd better take Maria with you," her mother, Amalia Tuitza, advised, giving me a concerned look. "He knew her when she was a baby and loves her. Unless she's with you, why would he trust you?"

"When you travel away from your own territory," Juan Arcos added, "men without women are considered to be killers. What would take you there, if not a headhunting raid?"

"Imagine that!" I turned to Juan Gabriel. "Men without women are warriors out to make a killing. It's like corporate America, all the way!"

It was agreed that Maria would accompany us. I must admit to a feeling of relief that went beyond the concern expressed by Juan Arcos; for me there was comfort in having a woman with us, especially one as attractive and nurturing as Yajanua Maria. She had been raised in Miazal, studied plant medicine under her mother's expert tutelage, and then, like Peem and some of her other siblings, traveled to Quito, where she had received a degree in nursing at the university. Later, she had dated a Peace Corps volunteer stationed for a year in Miazal and had lived with him in Tallahassee after he returned to the United States to complete graduate work at Florida State University. She was, in my opinion, an amazing woman, beautiful in so many ways, who managed to stay balanced while keeping one foot in the ancient world of arutam and one in the modern world of science.

My thoughts returned to the legendary warrior I hoped to meet somewhere out there in the remote rain forest. "Tukupi only killed Achuar?" I asked.

"Mostly, but sometimes other Shuar, too, from clans that were his family's enemies."

I confessed that I had wanted to meet Tukupi ever since I first heard about him, nearly three decades earlier. Even then, in the late 1960s, his reputation was legendary. He had been taking heads since the 1920s and had participated in the last of the great battles when, it was rumored, four hundred Shuar warriors marched against a fortified Achuar community. Now I would finally get my chance.

▲

Daniel Wachapa wandered into Miazal two days before Ehud's scheduled arrival. Although young by uwishin standards, his extraordinary life experiences more than compensated for his lack in years. He had been orphaned at a very early age when his parents were killed by a rival shaman. Largely self-taught, he had initiated himself into the shamanic world through taking a series of teacher-plant-induced journeys that had led him to a realization that his mission in life was to share the knowledge of his people with a world he had never even seen. Now in his late forties, he was dedicated to working with the Dream Change groups, teaching us about ayahuasca and tobacco, shapeshifting, and dream change. He and Eve Bruce had developed a strong personal relationship; as healers, they were fascinated with each other's philosophies and techniques.

"So Evita's writing a book?" Daniel smiled broadly. We sat together on a high embankment overlooking the Tsuirim River.

"And I'm sure you're in it."

"Not the first time I've appeared in print," he chuckled.

"You're right—I beat her to it. But hers will be very different from mine."

"More about healing." He picked up a flat stone and turned it in his fingers. "And now you're off to see Tukupi. . . ."

"In a couple of days, as soon as Ehud joins us."

"What an adventure!"

"Want to come?"

The look on his face told me he'd love to join us—but then he shook his head. "I've been gone from home a long time . . . too long." He cocked his arm and threw the stone toward the river. From this high angle it seemed impossible, but when the stone hit the water, it skipped along the surface, leaving a chain of silver circles in its wake. He looked at me and grinned. "But you can tell me all about it."

We sat in silence for a long time, listening to the sounds of the river and the forest. It took me back to another afternoon a year earlier, when Stephan Rechtschaffen and I had sat in this very spot. Stephan was an M.D. by training who, in 1977, had cofounded and was president of the Omega Institute, which—with over 20,000 students each year—had grown to become the largest holistic learning center in the United States. Also the author of the groundbreaking book, *Timeshifting,* he had brought his two sons on the trip to Ecuador with him—a high school graduation gift for Daniel and a college graduation gift for Rahmiel. As we reclined on the bank of the Tsuirim, he confided that he was deeply impressed by the wisdom of the shamans and the spirit of the Shuar. He proposed that Omega and DCC join forces to create an annual gathering of shamans at the Omega campus in upstate New York. It had become a reality. Daniel Wachapa would soon be participating in the first gathering. Along with the other shamans, he would also attend meetings in California and at a medical school in Ann Arbor, Michigan.

Now, as Daniel and I sat there together, I wondered what it would be like for him—not just the experience of traveling to a land and culture so different from his own but also the conference itself. What kinds of questions might he expect? I tried to frame one in my mind, and then I asked him, "What do you think is going to happen to us—to mankind—and to the world we're affecting so strongly?"

"I've only lived in a small part of it," he said. "Here, in this jungle."

"But that will change."

"Yes. Actually, it already has." He then described a shamanic journey he had taken to the Pacific Ocean and another he'd taken to Ann Arbor. His visions had been incredibly accurate. I long ago learned the power of such experiences and am seldom surprised by what people tell me. Yet, given that Daniel had never been to the ocean or a city—at least his physical body hadn't—even by shamanic standards his descriptions were extraordinarily detailed. Finally he returned to our starting point. "So, to answer your question about the future of mankind. . . . "

"Yes. Where are we headed?"

"We're like a warrior who's pulled his canoe onto a beach in an area unknown to him. He gets out and walks to the edge of the forest. It's dense, impossible to penetrate unless he's willing to spend days hacking a trail with his machete. He moseys a little farther up the beach and arrives at a place where two paths lead into the jungle. They veer off at different angles, obviously headed toward two completely separate and unknown locations. Which trail will he take?"

"How does he choose?"

"Hard to say, isn't it?" Daniel paused and pointed up the river. A large branch was hurtling down the rapids toward us, one leafy arm pointing high into the air. On this limb, perched like a delicate child upon a wild stallion, was a fragile lavender orchid. "What that warrior doesn't know is that one of those paths leads directly to a hostile village. Take that and he's done for!" The branch and orchid flew past us. "Like that orchid, how can the warrior know what fate awaits him?"

"But what if the warrior has a pretty good idea that one path would take him to his enemies? What if there were signs—tracks—indicating this?"

"Then of course he would take the other." He laughed. "I see it now—what you're getting at. I've learned from you and Eve, and from some of the others you bring here, that some of you are seeing those tracks. You know that if you continue along the path you've been taking, you're doomed."

"We're all doomed—including the Shuar."

"It's very simple, then. We must choose the other path."

"But how?" I knew what the branch and orchid in the wild river were headed for—and how little chance there was of their fate changing.

"That's why we're all here together, Shuar and gringos—to answer that question."

"What Dream Change is about."

He nodded and held up a twist of Shuar tobacco. "Dream on it."

Facing Fear with the Power of Arutam

Before leaving for his family, Daniel prepared a small cup of tobacco and gave it to me, and that night Juan Gabriel and I took it.

After we went to bed, I dreamed I was that warrior arriving on the beach in a canoe. I saw the two paths, but I couldn't make up my mind as to which was the right one. Finally, even though I had no clarity, I stepped forward and headed down the one on the right. Following it, I arrived at a stream cluttered with dead fish. Along the bank were heaps of rotting animal carcasses. Beyond them, the land was barren, littered with decaying tree trunks. My heart sank; I knew I had made the wrong choice. Then I spied one green branch reaching toward the sun, and on it sat a lavender orchid. The branch turned slowly toward me until the orchid pointed at the trail I had taken. Terrified that I had run out of time, I raced back along the trail, frantically retracing my steps. Suddenly, as I rounded a corner, a great jaguar confronted me, blocking the trail. It opened its mouth and let out a deafening roar.

"Aruuutam!" The jaguar's sound reverberated through the jungle.

▲

The next day, Ehud arrived, and he, Juan Gabriel, and I decided to spend time with Tuntuam, an old friend who was also a powerful and highly respected uwishin. We were interested in learning his opinion of Tukupi and his views about arutam, reincarnation, and the relationships between the Shuar and Achuar.

We crossed the swollen Mangosiza River by dugout canoe late in the afternoon. Once across and resting in the shade of a huge kapok tree, we were rewarded by a flock of parrots flying overhead, chattering loudly as they passed above our resting place. Juan Gabriel commented that they were welcoming us and were a good omen for the trip to come. The view was spectacular; the sun was setting behind the Cutucú Mountains, casting a blood-red ribbon across the river. It took me back to nights when I had sat with my parents around a fire in our New Hampshire home while we took turns reading out loud stories from our family's past, especially the forewarnings of Indian raids perceived in an exceptionally bright sunset, a crimson ring around the moon, or a vermilion streak across the water. I couldn't help but wonder which omens were true, the parrots or the ribbon on the river.

Tuntuam's longhouse was medium-sized by Shuar standards, an oval about twenty by fifty feet, constructed with great care of split palm staves pounded into the hard-packed earth with just enough space between them to ensure that no one on the outside could see in, yet providing those within with a perfect view of the clearing, the forests on three sides, and the trail that wound its way up from the river.

Tuntuam was waiting inside for us in the traditional manner of a kakaram warrior. He sat on a stool in the center of his home, before a blazing fire. In one hand he held a spear and in the other his single-shot, muzzle-loaded rifle, a prized gift from a man who had once insulted him and had presented him with this weapon in order to win clemency—and save his life. Tuntuam was wearing only a loincloth and a headdress made of brightly colored toucan feathers. His face was painted in crimson designs, and a permanent blue tattoo was etched across the bridge of his nose. He was a contemporary of Chumpi but was taller and thinner. Like so many of his generation, he wore his jet black hair cut straight across the forehead.

After the greetings, a welcoming dance, and the preparation of the ayahuasca we would take together later that night, he invited us to sit with him and called for one of his two wives to bring us chicha. We exchanged news and told him about our plans.

"Tukupi." He spoke the name slowly. He repeated it and nodded his head reverently. "It's been many years since I've seen him." His wrinkled face broke into a smile. "He's as old as the mountains." He laughed. "As old as me. I'm amazed he's still alive!"

"Before we go to the Forbidden Territory," I said, "we hoped to hear your thoughts about war, arutam, and the Achuar."

Tuntuam spoke to us at length, and we listened, a rapt audience in the light of his words. Since he had granted Ehud permission to videotape our meeting, we were all aware that they would be heard by many more people than the three of us.

"War is another test. Really it's a question of fears—how we face them, how we move through the cliff that blocks our way. Do we try to scale it, find a route around it, chisel our way through it, or simply stop and then turn back, like hunting dogs running home, whimpering and tripping over our own tails?

"We must always face our fears. We know there are many options but the only one that makes life worth living is to dominate those things we're afraid of. Sometimes our fears come in the form of jaguars, or it could be the anaconda—or the lightning itself. What's important is that we confront them, reach out to them when they appear during ayahuasca journeys, and face them when they leap out at us in everyday life.

"Avoiding fears, detouring around risks—these are for cowards, and they get us nowhere. What is this life about, anyway? It doesn't matter whether you're a warrior marching into battle or a woman whose child is dying of illness. You might be looking at demons within your soul. These things—all of them—can defeat us, even as an enemy soldier might kill us with the quick lunge of his spear."

Tuntuam shifted on his stool and leaned in for emphasis before he continued. "Finding arutam. There's the answer. That's what we each must do. We must look our fears straight in the eye—not shrink, but attack. Attack! The warrior is our model, the man who is kakaram. For men, it's what we seek. Women must also conquer their fears, but in a different way."

He leaned back and surveyed the three of us around him. "You know the story about Etsaa and the giant anaconda who lived at the bottom of the lake?" We shook our heads. "No? I'll tell you then. It happened long ago, before Etsaa became the sun, before the Evias invaded our lands. In those times there was a huge female anaconda, as big as if you strung as many canoes together as there are fingers on your hands and toes on your feet, placing them end to end. Can you imagine an anaconda so big?

"At night she rose out of the lake, in the blackest moment of the night, and crawled through the forest. She entered the longhouses of the Shuar people living in this area and devoured them. In the morning, neighbors would come around and find no one there. But they knew. Everyone did, for she would leave a huge trail in the dirt through the forest, the markings of her gigantic belly filled with the cadavers of our friends, bigger than the paths made by our people. It always led to the river, right down to a bank close to the place where the two rivers meet and form a lake. This lake was so deep that when people dropped into it rocks attached to vines, they never hit bottom. Even the longest vines ran out and slipped through their hands before the rocks found the bottom, as though there was no end, nothing down there but more water—and somewhere that giant anaconda. Lurking. Waiting. Filling the hearts of the bravest of our brave warriors with terror.

Tuntuam took a sip of chicha to wet his lips. "One morning Etsaa awoke to discover that his sister and her entire family were gone—she and her husband, his amikri, and all their little ones, the children he had played with and loved as though they were his very own—all of them eaten by that wretched anaconda. It was more than Etsaa could tolerate. He walked to the edge of the lake, followed by other brave warriors, but, once there, said to them, 'I must go alone, for it's not with numbers and weapons that we'll kill this terrible monster—only arutam will do it. I know now that this anaconda is here as a test. She can only be defeated when one of us overcomes all fear and descends into that lake alone, leaving all misgivings behind, unconcerned for what the next life brings, full of hope that it will be better, even, than this one, which is a glorious life. Only then can we put an end to this tragedy, to the suffering our cowardice has made us endure for too long.'

"With that he dove into the lake. Oh, how those waters shook! What waves! All of us Shuar thought Etsaa's days had ended. By nightfall, when he hadn't returned, we gave up and headed home, filled with despair. Not one of us could forget his words, though, for we knew he was right. It was fear and fear alone that was our enemy. We understood the meaning of arutam as we had never understood it before. We vowed to one another, we men, that we each would descend into that lake and fight the anaconda. We would kill her, or the entire Shuar people would die trying."

He set down his chicha, sat up straight, and rested his hands on his thighs. "You know the end." He laughed softly and nodded. "Several days later, Etsaa returned, carrying the skin of that loathsome anaconda. He had been victorious. We'd been prepared to keep our promises, but it wasn't necessary. Etsaa had saved the day. We set a great feast, with lots of chicha, dancing, and lovemaking. Etsaa tossed the anaconda's skin into the night sky where you can see it outlined in the stars to this day. And we learned our lessons about overcoming fears, about the power of arutam.

"So, you see why we fight. As I told you, to dominate our fears. But since that time of Etsaa and the anaconda, we've found other reasons, too. We also kill each other because our blood and that of our enemies fertilizes the earth. When we die we make room for the next generations. Our corpses nourish the plants."

Other Lives

Ehud asked Tuntuam to wait while he changed the cartridge in his camera. The old uwishin watched him carefully, then, when Ehud had finished, he pointed, smiling, at the lens and resumed talking.

"You know that when a man dies, no one will shoot an animal seen walking near his house. Even a tapir or a boar—favorite foods. Why? Because it's likely that the dead man's spirit is in that animal."

I spoke up then, "So really, there is no death?"

"No. We don't die, we just become something else. When a warrior kills another man, he does that man a favor, allowing him to move on. That's the reason for protecting animals wandering in the forests near the homes of dead men. The old uwishin used to tell us that the human shape is not one of the best, that we come as men to learn certain things, lessons, and yet we're happier as the ayahuasca vine or the jaguar.

"If I stab another man with my spear, in honest battle, killing him quickly, I help him shapeshift into his next life. I've served him well. Knowing this, why would a warrior fear death? Why would I? Or you?"

This time Ehud asked a question. "Does the shrinking of heads hinder this shapeshifting, maybe keep a man from changing into the form he'll have in his next life?"

Tuntuam smiled at first at Ehud's thought but then looked directly at him and leaned forward as if to show he took the question seriously. "Why do we shrink heads? There are several reasons. One is to bring peace to the slain man's soul. Another is to capture his vengeful spirit and keep it inside that tsantsa so it will not come back to haunt the warrior who defeated him. And still another, to bring him home to our families and perform the ceremonies, the ritual dances, and feasts, allowing the spirit to join us. Shrinking heads helps shapeshifting—it doesn't hinder it at all.

"Now, the last thing you asked about when we began talking was the difference between the Achuar and the Shuar, and so I'll tell you. You know the story about Etsaa showing the Shuar how to defeat the Evias by trickery? Remember, he taught the Shuar to make traps in the forests and poison the meat and chicha he brought to the Evias? The Shuar had never been this way before, sneaky and clever. Until then we'd always confronted our enemies head on, face to face. Etsaa taught us that sometimes when the enemy is too strong, we need to rely on our minds, our cleverness.

"Finally, all the Evias died, and Etsaa flew right up there into the sky, where we can see him and thank him every day. We feel his energy and his love. He reminds us what it means to be kakaram, to have arutam and also to use our knowledge, not just our bodies—to be smart.

"So what is the difference between the Achuar and the Shuar? Well, they didn't have to deal with the Evias in the same way we did. They live farther away from the Cutucú. They never learned to use their heads. So, today, when our warriors fight the Achuar, we attack them from ambush. They stand there in the open waiting to die. Our men, kakaram men like Tukupi, that valiant warrior you'll soon meet, kill them quickly, sending them on their way to their next life.

"I've heard the Achuar call kakaram men like Tukupi cowards because we fight with our heads, use the knowledge that Etsaa shared with us. They can call us anything they want, but, you know what? We think the way they fight is just plain stupid."

Tuntuam paused and nodded firmly. With this final opinion expressed, it seemed he had finished his teaching and explaining for the time being. We were all left to our own thoughts in the firelight. I mused that the uwishin's story of Etsaa and the giant anaconda reminded me of the ancient Anglo-Saxon legend of Beowulf. I recounted the story for Tuntuam. Like Etsaa, this medieval warrior had been called upon to kill the monster Grendel, who had been devouring the people of King Hrothgar's kingdom. He arrived by boat, coming from across the water, a magnificent warrior. Once he had accomplished his heroic task, the kingdom celebrated, holding a banquet in Beowulf's honor and presenting him with great treasures. There was feasting, singing, and dancing, and the mead flowed.

The hero Beowulf planned to return home the following morning, but during the night another monster arrived—Grendel's mother. She rose up from the depths of a bottomless lake and killed Hrothgar's best friend, a renowned warrior. The king pleaded with Beowulf to rid the kingdom of this terrible new menace. Beowulf went to the lake, accompanied by all his warriors as well as those of Hrothgar, but once there he turned to them and announced that he would go it alone, that they must wait behind. They complied with his wishes, and several days passed before he emerged from the water victorious.

Tuntuam didn't seem surprised at the similarities between the story of Etsaa and the epic of Beowulf. "I think," he said, "that warriors around the world are the same. We realize that all battles are fought more in the heart than with weapons and brute strength. We know that despite the closeness of our comrades, in the end it's always up to each of us alone. No matter how valiant he is or how many heads he has previously taken, no warrior ever knows the outcome of his next battle. Will he win?" He thrust his spear into the fire for a moment, then removed it and touched his finger to the hot point. "It really doesn't matter. The fire is all that's important, the heat of our passion. That's arutam. To charge into the fray, give it everything you've got. Success is not whether you win or lose, but that you fought with all your heart."

Tukupi

Yajanua Maria, Ehud, Juan Gabriel, and I sat before a night fire in Tukupi's longhouse. His two wives passed chicha as he told us stories and chanted into the microphone that was strapped to an old spear set in the ground before his stool. Outside, frogs croaked and monkeys howled until, off in the distance, the occasional scream of a jaguar pierced the darkness, momentarily transforming the raucous jungle into a tomb of deathly silence.

Tukupi, his silhouette dancing high in the rafters, tattooed face illuminated by the flickering light, described some of the many enemies he had slain, the anents sung, and heads shrunk to ward off vengeful spirits as well as irate family members. He talked openly of his own fear—"I never left the house, not even to pick a banana from the palm outside my door, without my spear or gun; I was ever vigilant, my heart hammering against my ribs like a woodpecker on a tree whenever I left my home." And he spoke of the arutam that helped him overcome it—"My ancestors came to me, anaconda men who slithered down tree trunks and hardened my heart."

In the light of the fire we listened, rapt, to the experiences of this man whose reputation echoed throughout the forest, far beyond his home. His accounts of bravery and strength in the face of the enemy's challenge painted our imaginations with the colors of glistening skin and bright blood against a background of vivid green. Our occasional exchange of glances communicated the same thing: Each of us was glad we came to Tukupi in friendship.

One of his tales recounted the time an Achuar warrior sent a messenger to him with a challenge. "The messenger told me I was a lazy old lout who spent my days doing nothing but making love with women." Tukupi smiled and went on. "I sent a song back to him. 'Test my prowess, old man,' my song said to him." He looked at us and laughed. "He did it—he came to get me. I waited in the bushes until it was time, then I leaped out at him. You should've seen his face! The shock, the fear! I raised my spear. He lunged at my heart and missed. *He* should have made love to women more often! It would've honed his reflexes. I killed him." He took a sip of chicha and wiped the residue from his lips. "Then I sent word to his clan: 'If you try to avenge his death,' I warned his brothers, 'I'll shapeshift into a huge snake and wipe out all of you, transform you into rodents. I am an anaconda man.'"

That one night with Tukupi was filled with a lifetime of legends from a man who was himself a living legend. His stories recalled my favorite boyhood books of heroism—*The Last of the Mohicans*, *Drums Along the Mohawk*, and *Ivanhoe*—connecting the threads of my culture's perception of strength and bravery with the heroism I was discovering among the Shuar. I was aware of how privileged we were to be able to spend such time with this great warrior who had long ago traded his spear for the shaman's tumank.

Not only did the stories themselves hold our attention, but, like the greatest of the troubadours, Tukupi was a master of delivery who played his stories in many keys. He possessed an amazing ability to disarm his listeners by turning his own legendary exploits into tales that were funny and poignant but never boastful. He was quick to laugh at himself—which made him, to us, a very human hero.

The details of his adventures and his manner of relating them were singular, yet the context echoed our conversations with Domingo, Tutuam, Chumpi, and other uwishin men. Like them, Tukupi attributed all his prowess to arutam and to the spirits of the forest who walk beside the Shuar day and night.

As the fire burned, we listened to the words this uwishin gave us, wisdom on the importance of having faith and of following intuition and the dictates of the heart, what he referred to as "the Voice of the Universe." Touching his chest, he smiled and said, "Your heart is part of the universe. It speaks to you all the time. You only have to listen."

Later that night, after the stories were over and the chicha pots dry, while everyone was sleeping, I crawled out of my blanket and headed into the clearing around the longhouse. The sky was alive with stars. A firefly flickered here and there among the trees. Slowly I walked into the dark, drawn by what I thought of as the Voice of the Universe.

Suddenly I froze. A blue light flashed high up in the canopy. Then it rose out of the forest, a vibrating globe of blue energy, hovering just over the trees. Almost immediately another light appeared, rising above the dark forest, seeming to materialize out of the air itself, until the two lights hovered side by side. After a moment of suspension, they rushed toward me and then, before I had time to react, quickly retreated, disappearing behind the thick wall of trees. It all happened very quickly. I stood there for what seemed a long time. Finally I returned to the longhouse and fell into a deep sleep.

In the morning, I told Tukupi about my experience with the blue globes.

"Chumpi," he said, grinning, referring to the shaman who had just passed out of his human form, as he had predicted he would.

"Chumpi? That was Chumpi?"

He nodded enthusiastically.

"They weren't extraterrestials? From another planet? A star?"

"Yes, yes." He assured me they were extraterrestrials and also the shaman. "We're all one," he said. His two hands touched my heart.*

* For more on Tukupi (also known as Tampur), the Voice of the Universe, and the blue globes, see *Shapeshifting*, Destiny Books, Rochester, VT, chapters 14 and 16.

Shapeshifting

in the Words of

Mariano, Chumpi, Tuntuam, Daniel Wachapa, Domingo, and Peem

Through Death

Mariano: In the past, before the arrival of the missionaries, our grandparents knew that people never die; their spirits shapeshift into animals, plants, or waterfalls.

When a person shapeshifted, his body wasn't removed like today. Instead, it was left in the house so that love for the person could be shown by always keeping a fire or candle burning at his side. The relatives also left a bowl of chicha beside him so he wouldn't be thirsty or hungry. The morning after, they would discover that all the chicha had been drunk by the dead person's spirit. I've heard about this so many times!

After the proper period of time had passed and the spirit had transformed into the body of an animal, plant, or waterfall, a burial of the cadaver would take place. Instead of a coffin, they used a hollow tree or canoe, sealed with beeswax caulking on the outside. If there were bugs inside the tree, all the better—they would keep the spirit company during this time of transition. Finally, the body was buried and completely covered with earth.

No one is meant to stay in the world forever as a human; we all must shapeshift. Our grandparents knew this. They wanted to make the transition easy, and they wanted to keep the spirit from coming to them in their dreams and telling them he was hungry—that's why they left food. They feared that the spirit would haunt them if they didn't show him the proper respect and love.

The death of a family member is painful for those left behind. It makes life difficult for men when their women die. Who will prepare chicha and take care of the children? When a man dies, who will hunt and protect the home? We fast after a family member dies, and then later, maybe after several days, we may eat parts of the chonta palm. Chonta is the hardest wood because it has a hard life. This makes it a fitting symbol for what we feel when a loved one leaves us. We have to remember, however, that the person hasn't disappeared, only shapeshifted into another form. When my sister left, we all mourned her and felt terribly sorry for her children; but we knew she was happy because during our initiation we had experienced her shapeshift and understood that she had arrived in a wonderful place.

In the old days everyone realized that a person who left this human life could pass his powers on to his children. When ancestors shapeshifted into the anaconda or jaguar, they could also share some of their arutam with the ones left behind. All people who die can transform themselves—women and men alike—into the jaguar, the anaconda, or the boar. Animals can also transform and give us arutam—all animals have this power. So do the elements. For example, Nase, the wind, has great arutam power. Whenever Nase blows through the forest, the old ones tell the younger ones to go out and walk among the trees. It's a frightening thing to do! The noise of the wind and thunder is deafening, and all around, trees crash down in the forest. But people do it just the same. My amikri John has done it. It impressed all the Shuar so much that we gave him the name "Nase."

Our grandparents knew how to disappear into the wind and when they disappeared they escaped from the rain. It was what we call being in the dream, living the dream. That's the essence of shapeshifting.

Chumpi: I can tell you a shapeshifting story about a young woman from way over on the other side of the ocean.* She was in very bad shape; her condition was life threatening. She didn't need a physical healing; she needed a shapeshift—when John and Juan Gabriel brought her to me, I could see that right away. Nothing was wrong physically, but spiritually she was a goner! She wanted to die.

---

*A Japanese student who was part of a DCC group of twelve college students organized by St. Thomas University in Miami.

I had taken ayahuasca, of course, but she hadn't. Her group leader said they couldn't take it.* I thought: How strange! Ayahuasca is the best teacher for our children. However, I honored their decisions.

As soon as I started journeying for her, I really flew. Very high. I went far away and met an old woman, an angry old lady who shook her fist at me. "I'm her grandmother," she said.

"You've shapeshifted," I said.

"Dead, you mean?" She laughed, and her breath smelled of the grave. Then her face became mean. "Don't be ridiculous," she yelled at me.

Juan Gabriel was translating to the young woman as fast as he could. She confirmed that her grandmother had deserted her human body three years before. Crying, she told us that she couldn't forget the old woman, that her grandmother haunted her.

"Leave that young girl alone," I told the old lady, that dark shadow spirit.

"She's mine," the old woman screamed. "I want her back!"

I knew then that there would be trouble. "Not now," I told her. "She's too young, she's not ready for that shapeshift yet—it's not her time."

I saw the old wretch reach out to seize the poor girl. I flew into the girl's place and grabbed and shook the old woman. She shoved me off, causing me to fall and nearly crack my head.

The wretch cackled and gave me a terrifying scowl. "Okay," she said. "If not her, then you!" She put her hands on me—cold hands. "You're old, you can come with me. If it isn't her time, it's yours!"

I was very scared. I asked Juan and John to hold my hands, to keep me firmly in this world. They did it right away.

Suddenly, the young woman spoke up. "I want to see my grandmother again," she said. "But many years in the future, when I die—not now."

*College policy prohibited it.

I repeated this for the old lady and added, "You can't have me, either. Your granddaughter agrees to come to you later, many years from now, after she's completed what she came into this life to do."

That grandmother released me and laughed. I could see that her teeth were broken. "Fair enough," she said, and began to fade out of sight. "But, remember, I'll hold her to her bargain—and you, too, old Chumpi!"

Well, that same night, I knew for sure that I would shapeshift into the bat soon, that I didn't have many days left in this life of mine as a Shuar man. I told John and Juan Gabriel all about that and John asked if he could record this story on his little machine. So I said yes. Now, he tells me he is *giving* me the machine! I'll enjoy it these last days, listening to my own music that he recorded once before. Then I'll be a bat and have no more use for the little machine.*

With North American Shamans

Tuntuam: There is a woman named Maria who works with John†
and brings groups here. She's learned to live among us and has
become a good friend. She tells me that she's taken our custom of
shrinking heads back to her people, where she uses it to shapeshift
warriors who are haunted by the enemies they've killed. She says
that her country never before had an effective way to deal with
those vengeful spirits until she learned it from the Shuar. Since
the tsantsa is not part of their traditions, they don't actually shrink
the head of the slain enemy; they shrink something else instead and
bury it, putting inside it the spirit that haunts the warrior, laying it
to rest. I'm happy that this ancient Shuar ritual is helping others.
Maria is a shapeshifter who applies Shuar wisdom to bring arutam
to her warriors!

---

* The story of how Chumpi (also known as Kitiar) shapeshifted into a bat is told in detail in *Shapeshifting*, Destiny Books, Rochester, VT: 1997, chapter 11.

†Tuntuam is referring to DCC trip facilitator and licensed psychotherapist Mary Tendall, whose clinical work focuses on Vietnam veterans.

Daniel Wachapa: The ways I heal people are very different from those of medical doctors in the United States. Doctor Eve Bruce is a good friend of mine— a medical doctor from the United States who does her work there. She and I have spent many hours together and have learned much from each other. She's told me about the methods U.S. doctors use. Our techniques may be different, but I can tell you this—my Shuar ways work. They are powerful! Both Eve and John have been healed by me and have seen me heal many of their people of a variety of diseases. I'm sure Eve's ways also work. She's a powerful woman. I think the two methods are complementary, though Eve tells me that she's convinced that mine are better in many cases.

For example, she was deeply impressed when I brought hearing back to a deaf woman who came here with her.* It was a classic case of changing the dream, shapeshifting. Eve told me that the woman had been deaf for about twenty years and that the medical doctors had tried everything without success. Here in the jungle it took only one night!

Another time a doctor in her country wanted to amputate John's leg—it was badly infected—but John came to me first. I was certain I could cure it—not me, really, but the ayahuasca, the volcano, and the anaconda. And we succeeded—in one night. That's how I work, shapeshifting into the volcano or the anaconda and using the elements and spirits to help me. I really don't do anything; the work is done by the arutam, the forces of nature.

---

*This refers to the well-documented story of Sara Aboulhosn, researcher in a U.S. pharmaceutical laboratory, who became totally deaf at ten years old with a rare illness known as Cogan's Syndrome, which, according to medical texts, is nearly always permanent. She regained much of her hearing during a trip to Daniel Wachapa in 1999 when she was thirty-five, and her balance during a 2000 DCC workshop in Florida—in front of seventy-five people. See, for example, Ann Japenga, "Eve Bruce: Meet the Beauty Mystic," *Health* magazine, September 2000, pp. 197–98.

With Black Shamans

Mariano: Black shamans also used shapeshifting in the past. When people had taken datura or ayahuasca, a black shaman might appear as a jaguar. He knew all kinds of witchcraft and could turn people into stone, or kill or maim a person. These shamans spread evil energy by blowing on people—thousands died this way in the past. It still happens, but not so much today.

One of the reasons black shamanism has died out is that the old wars have stopped. You see, it was really used against enemies. And whether something was black shamanism or not was a matter of perspective; what one family saw as black shamanism another family might see as something good that protected them from their enemy.

Domingo: Shapeshifting could be a great help to warriors. Anyone can see how it could work to make a warrior stronger or even invisible. The shamans guided the arutam for warriors. Black shamanism was definitely part of warfare—and frequently it was the cause of hatred between two clans since it was also practiced for revenge. If a man's child or wife died, and the shaman did not save his or her life, or the person died because of the shaman's work, he became known as a black shaman and was punished. The father of a child who had died might seize and kill the bad shaman.

Mariano: Now practically no real shamans are like that. They work through the study of good energy, avoiding black magic.

For Seduction

Peem: Once there was a Shuar couple, and the man and woman were very happy and contented. Uncharacteristically, the woman had no interest in other men, not even younger ones. Eventually, however, the man began to get lazy. He even neglected to bring in wood for the kitchen fires. This disappointed the woman.

One afternoon, the couple returned home to find the kitchen full of firewood. The man was as surprised as his wife. Who could have done this? He became suspicious of her, convinced that she had taken up with another man, even though he had seen no signs of her infidelity.

The husband decided to spy on his wife. He crept through the forests, following her, watching her every move. He hid in the bushes near the yucca garden and peeked through the kitchen walls. Try as he might, though, he could find no evidence to prove his theory—except that every day another pile of fresh firewood mysteriously appeared in the kitchen. He began to accuse his wife, and when she defended herself, the tranquility of their home broke down into fits of arguing.

The woman was as confused as her husband. But she was aware of something he knew nothing about: Every night she had beautiful, erotic dreams. A handsome man whom she had known when she was younger came to her, and they made love together all night long.

Meanwhile, the husband decided it was time to talk with his friends about what was happening. He learned that others had had similar experiences. He also discovered that a handsome man from far away had been seen in the neighborhood. It was said that this man could shapeshift himself into a larva in order to sneak into houses and make love with the women. One of the friends advised the husband, "Around midnight, take a torch and search under your bed. If you find a larva attached to it, kill it. That will end this story!"

The man followed his friend's advice—and indeed, he found a large larva clinging to the bottom of the bed, right under the place where his wife was sleeping. He knocked it to the floor and immediately killed it, and that put an end to the handsome man who had learned how to shapeshift into a larva in order to sneak past men and seduce women.

This is an old tale, part of Shuar mythology, but even today we believe there is truth in it. Both men and women can shapeshift into a larva and make love with someone of the opposite sex. For that reason, we're careful. We make a point of sleeping with a spouse or a friend we trust—and we always check under the bed to see whether a larva is lurking there!

The Sacred Teacher Plants

Always fascinating to the people who attended our DCC workshops and to those who went on our trips were the Shuar's three sacred teacher plants: ayahuasca, tobacco, and datura. The attitudes of these people were representative of a widespread cultural obsession with such things—one flavored with both suspicion and curiosity. They almost always referred to these plants as "drugs" and "hallucinogens." I vehemently disputed these references because, from the Shuar point of view, the three plants do not have the characteristics we generally associate with the substances in either of these categories.

Bob Southard, Lyn's associate editor at *Dream Change Magazine,* often assisted Eve and me at our workshops. As a businessman, his persona was opposite that of someone who might be considered part of a drug culture. He had, however, spent time with the Shuar and experienced ayahuasca and tobacco. During a Boston workshop I called on him to share his perspective.

"For the Shuar," Bob explained, "these plants open the doors to understanding greater realities. They're not taken to escape, but rather so the Shuar can go deeper and experience enhanced understanding." He paused and smiled. "I think the Shuar might consider television hallucinogenic, since it separates us from reality. The teacher plants are at the other end of the spectrum. I can tell you from personal experience that the lessons are not always fun. You get what you need. Sometimes that means facing things you've been trying to avoid or deny."

Eve, who was also present at the workshop, spoke up then. "I'd like to say that anything used by indigenous people for thousands of years has to be taken seriously. When we talk about the use of drugs in our culture, we're talking about recreational use. This form of recreation is unknown to indigenous cultures. In a tribe people are always working, always playing. There isn't a clear distinction between the two. Both are part of living life as a human. By comparison, in our culture we look to recreation as a means to escape our everyday work and concerns, to escape what we consider reality.

"I have a great deal of personal experience living with someone who has an addiction to alcohol. It's been my observation that it's not the spirit (alcohol) that causes the problem, but the lack of spirituality; it's not the substance itself, but the person's intent behind his or her use. The intent of an addict is to disconnect, to escape. Over time, this disconnection becomes the reality, and dysfunction in that person's community is the unfortunate long-term consequence. In a tribal community—especially in the jungle—addiction isn't an option. It doesn't happen. You would die if you disconnected and became dysfunctional. The intent in ritual use, even of very dangerous and temporarily debilitating substances such as datura and ayahuasca, is to connect more deeply, rather than to escape. Their desire is to learn and to find ways to expand reality through this deeper connection long after the biochemical effect of the substance has abated."

"To me," Bob added, "there's no connection between these plants and their synthetic counterparts such as LSD. Like Eve, I'm struck by the fact that cultures across the entire vast Amazon basin have used these three plants for longer than anyone can know. Indigenous people throughout the world embrace other plants in similar rituals."

I pointed out that many anthropologists believe North American tribes used datura, psilocybin in mushrooms, and other local plants to induce their vision quests and shamanic rituals, but that the knowledge of these was totally annihilated by the European—and later U.S.—military and missionaries. In fact, botanists theorize that a psychotropic tobacco similar to the Shuar's was favored by many tribes in their pipe ceremonies; they purposely chose to allow it to become extinct rather than share it with white invaders.

Psychotropic Plants and the Catholic Church

One of the Boston workshop participants asked how it had happened that such knowledge had been lost in North America but not in South America.

"There's the rather obvious reason that tribes like the Shuar live in very remote areas; they've never been conquered, so their culture has been kept whole." I went on to explain that even today Shuar territory is governed primarily by the Shuar Federation. "You never see a policeman inside that huge area; it's run very much as though it is a separate country outside the limits of Ecuadorian rule and also beyond the grasp of the United States and the United Nations."

Eve added, "All over the Ecuadorian Andes, growing in almost every convent and monastery and beside churches, you find psychotropic plants, the sacred teachers—especially datura, and mushrooms containing psilocybin, and San Pedro, the powerful cactus worshiped by many Mesoamerican cultures—species that thrive at high altitudes. In the markets you run across ayahuasca and tobacco brought up from the rain forests. Talk to some of the priests, and you'll learn that many of them use these plants." She turned to me. "Right?"

"Absolutely." I went on to describe several priests who were regular users of ayahuasca, tobacco, and San Pedro, including a Catholic missionary who swore that ayahuasca, in addition to providing relief for his arthritis, induced euphoric trance states that were profoundly spiritual in nature. "One priest," I added, "told me that, as far as he was concerned, such plants are part of the sacrament, a means for helping him to open up to the wonders of nature, Christ, and God."

When people expressed their surprise at this notion, I told them about a statue perched on the walls of a Catholic church in Cuenca, Ecuador's third largest city. "It depicts the baby Jesus rising out of a San Pedro cactus." I paused to let this sink in, then added, "It seems that while the English—and later the U.S.—government was bent on wiping out all aspects of indigenous cultures in their conquered lands, the Spanish were more concerned with exploiting local populations to produce textiles and other products to sell in Europe. It also appears that while my forefathers, New England Puritans and Calvinists, saw the devil in people who walked naked in the forests, the

Spanish Catholics saw opportunities for conversion. When you read North American colonial texts, the vehemence of Puritan hatred for indigenous ways is striking, as is their determination to rid the world of indigenous influence. The Spanish chronicles, however, stress the importance of allowing local populations to maintain their traditions—as long as individuals were baptized and attended Mass. This is reflected by the symbolism in the cathedrals and churches in parts of South America. Throughout Ecuador these buildings are decorated with carvings depicting indigenous notions of the sun god and moon goddess. One of the oldest colonial structures in the hemisphere—a cathedral in Quito—has an amazing statue of the Virgin Mary with wings spreading from her shoulders. This symbol of Christianity is poised to take a shamanic flight into the worlds of indigenous wisdom."

Someone stood up and described a coca ceremony she had attended in the Peruvian highlands. "It was incredibly beautiful and sacred. I couldn't believe how my culture has taken that plant and perverted it. The indigenous people respect it, they learn from it. We corrupt it, processing it, mixing other chemicals with it, and then turn it into a commercial agent of greed and addiction."

"Exactly the same for tobacco," another person added.

A grandmotherly woman with graying hair and glasses raised her hand. "I'm curious: Is it the processing and additives that make cocaine and tobacco so notoriously addictive in the United States? Here, in the case of tobacco, at least, the addiction is part of the physiological response to the nicotine. If the addictive ingredients of our cocaine and tobacco are present in the coca and tobacco of the indigenous people of South America, how do they avoid the biological responses of addiction or craving?"

I stepped forward. "I'm not sure I can answer your question except to say that in all the years I've worked with indigenous people, I haven't met one who is still part of his or her culture and is addicted—at least not that I am aware of. The caveat about being part of the culture may be the key. The issue of addiction is often entirely different for those who've either forsaken their culture or been forced from it for whatever reason—those who've moved into cities, become part of the white man's world and the urban way of life, which can lead to exposure to, and abuse of, drugs like processed cocaine, heroin, LSD, and hard liquor."

"The range of drug dependencies we see among North American indigenous people, for example," the woman offered.

"Yes. It's an interesting subject. A woman who's attended many of our workshops wrote her Harvard doctoral thesis on this subject. She discovered, among other things, that there's absolutely no scientific evidence to support the theory that indigenous people have any genetic or physical predisposition toward addiction or alcoholism—certainly no more so than the nonindigenous community. Addiction is often more a cultural and social issue."

"The shamans," Eve added, "always emphasize that the spirit of the plant and the intent of the user are what count, not its chemical composition."

Ayahuasca

When Shuar uwishin offered ayahuasca to trip participants, it was an opportunity that sometimes created dilemmas. People would agonize for days over whether or not to accept it. Our cultural biases had taught them that the possible reactions to "drugs" were either to be fearful of them or to crave them as a vehicle for escape or adventure, or as a panacea for emotional ills.

Several of the DCC trips were planned by a married couple who founded and managed Innervision, a Michigan-based organization dedicated to teaching new ways of looking at the world. Art Roffey and Gail Danto had hosted a number of my workshops and also had led their own groups to indigenous cultures in Peru. Art was a Ph.D. psychologist and had been a teacher of psychology at the Air Force Academy. He was also a visionary who had written articles and recorded CDs to help people reduce stress, take vision quests, and feel their closeness to nature. He, Gail, and Innervision supported DCC in many ways. Very aware of the dilemma facing many of the people he had brought, he requested that we have an opportunity to talk with members of the Shuar community prior to the ayahuasca ceremony.

One morning Mariano took us to his parents' home. As was customary, I introduced Art and the others, and we sat in the circle and drank chicha together. Then I explained our reasons for coming.

Domingo expressed his pleasure at our interest in the plants he and his family held in such high esteem. "Natem is a plant we worship, a powerful spirit, a god," he said. "The size of mature natem is equal to the large limbs of a full-grown tree. It is a creeping vine with bright green leaves that gives us arutam, shows us the way, and helps with many things, including raising animals, maintaining relationships with our spouses and families, and hunting. It's also a teacher for our children. This power of natem is beyond measure."

Art asked him to describe how it is prepared for human consumption.

"First, the vine is cut with a machete. It's taken home and the bark, which is thin, is peeled off. The stems are cut up, then mixed with the leaves of another plant, a lover spirit, such as yage. Water is poured into pots, then natem and the lover plant are added to the pots and are simmered for hours over the fire. All the elements are present here: earth, air, fire, and water. The scum is removed from the top when the liquid has boiled down, and then the pots are removed from the fire. We drink it after dark; sometimes, with just a shaman present, we take it very strong. This is at special times, when we need to be healed, to resolve some problem, or to have a disease or injury cured."

"That's the way you'll take it tonight," I said. I explained that it was always drunk after dark because it may make the eyes very sensitive, even resulting in powerful night vision. I also mentioned that neither Juan Gabriel nor I would take ayahuasca during the ceremony so that we could be fully present to assist the trip participants. "We are very familiar with it, though," I assured them. "Personally." This comment was met with a lot of laughter.

"At other times," Domingo continued, "we take a weaker form of natem as a community, or in our family circle. Boys and old men, girls and old women collect as many cups as they want to drink. We go to a sacred place, where we feel safe and one with the spirits and nature, accompanied by the tunduli [drum]. The person in charge and all the others drink three, four, or maybe six cups from the pot of natem—until they begin to journey into other worlds. Since they're journeying, they have the power of arutam. Arutam brings strength, wisdom, and good luck.

"The dizziness of natem passes by midnight, no later, and in the morning the participants don't appear to have taken natem at all." Then Domingo leaned back and smiled at the people, who had been listening intently.

Datura

"Maikiua," Mariano added, "what you call *datura,* is another sacred plant that's very important to us. It's a small bush with leaves that are always green

and gorgeous white flowers. The leaves are great healers for wounds when applied directly to the injured area in a poultice. If you see maikiua in the moonlight, you see something incredible."

"How is it prepared?" Art asked.

Domingo held up a hand, letting us know that he had already anticipated this question. "First, to use maikiua, the custom here is for a person to go to the beach. Once there, he scrapes the skin from the plant with a small knife. This portion of skin must not exceed the size of the smallest fingernail on the user's hand. It's that powerful! Just a tiny piece of the plant's skin does the trick! You dissolve this piece in water. When the sun is setting, the shaman takes the maikiua and also offers it to his patient—his son, wife, daughter, grandchild, or someone who has come to him for help. After half an hour, the patient is dizzy. Ah, I tell you!—it's good and strong, much more so than pure liquor when drunk straight."

"Are any special preparations necessary before taking datura," one of the members of Art's group asked, "like the fasting we do for ayahuasca?"

"Very similar," Domingo responded. "In order to take maikiua, you must not eat dinner, breakfast, or lunch. Don't eat anything at all for at least a full day and night. After you take it, your head aches; it throbs. You can't walk but rather remain stretched out on the ground. Even the shaman who may have taken it several times before has lost his senses and gone flying, like a crazy man. But he's not crazy—he journeys and is open to transformation and incredible shapeshifts. So are you."

"How do you feel then? What's it like?"

The old man continued. "Maikiua has the power of the anaconda and the arutam of the jaguar and all of nature. After receiving maikiua you must lie stretched out, senseless, in a trance for two or three days. At the end of that period, when someone asks how you feel and you answer that you feel well, everyone must be careful around you. We all must help by not letting you eat anything but salt, sugar, and a little water. You can't eat meat, fish, or yucca; you can't drink chicha or anything else for a week, until the maikiua has passed out of you. Maikiua is felt in the belly. To make it pass out fast, you must take salt water." Domingo paused

"You can see," Rosa Shakai interjected, "that maikiua is a very important teacher for us. It helps us look beyond the everyday world into the greater reality, to appreciate our arutam, our oneness with all that's around us."

"It is also extremely dangerous," I felt compelled to add. "Datura can kill any of us—even the Shuar. Unlike ayahuasca, it is never offered to people on our trips. Unless you decide to live with the Shuar for several years, you cannot even condsider tryng it."

When I translated, our three hosts all echoed my warnings. "Ayahuasca is the only one you might try," Mariano advised, "never datura!"

Chicha

Domingo turned to his wife. His blind eyes gave her his full appreciation. "She makes the best maikiua. Also chicha. If you want to learn about our ceremonies, then you have to understand about chicha. It is most important for all our beautiful ceremonies. In fact, chicha is our most sacred food and also the one we drink more than any other. We drink it all day long. People ask me if we ever get drunk from chicha." He laughed, and his wife and son joined in. "Well, how silly! Can you imagine a drunk man going to war or paddling a canoe down the rapids of the Mangosiza River? Or hunting a wild boar? Of course not."

"It doesn't sound like you can paddle a canoe after taking ayahuasca or datura either," one of our group stated, grinning.

"Oh, no." They all laughed some more. Then Domingo became serious. "When we take natem or maikiua, we do it in a safe place, at a designated time. Then we're what you might call drunk—we couldn't fight or hunt. But we drink chicha all the time. We feel very good from it, happy. Chicha makes us laugh! Afterward, we can walk on a tiny log, no bigger than your wrist, across a canyon, over swirling rapids. Do you call that drunk?"

Tina, a woman from Michigan who had been with Art on an earlier trip to Peru, spoke up. "This morning Amalia gave us a woman's perspective on how chicha is prepared. Could you tell us about chicha from a man's point of view?"

Domingo glanced at his wife. She was busy straining the beer through a gourd perforated with dozens of holes. "Only women are allowed to prepare chicha, or even to touch it; men may let it come in contact with only their lips, nothing else. The women start to make the chicha while the men are out hunting, very early in the morning, before Etsaa, the sun, has even awoken. They go out to the gardens and sing to Nunqui, goddess of the plants and earth, seeking her permission to dig up the yucca [manioc] roots. After receiving her blessings, they fill their *changuinas* [carrying baskets], then they replant the yucca, covering it well with Nunqui's soil so that it will shapeshift back into life as a new plant. The yucca teaches us about shapeshifting, that life never ends, there's always regeneration. The women tie up the baskets and sling the straps across their foreheads so the vessels lie across their backs and are supported by their strong necks and heads. All women know how to have them tied up high. Once they're home they peel and wash the yucca; then they boil it, and chew it, and spit it into the pots. After this the chicha is ready to ferment."

"In the time of our grandfathers, the chicha fiesta was incredible," Mariano observed. "And it still is."

Art said, with evident enthusiasm, "We'd love to hear about it!"

"Our grandfathers taught it to us, and we still practice it," Domingo said, and then he paused. He raised his head as if seeing a scene replayed in the air before him. "The women wore beautiful dancing belts. The men played flutes and drums. The oldest man decided when the dance should start, using a special flute, like a bird whistle, to get everything moving. After the music stopped, the couples rested and the dancing was finished. The only thing different these days is that we now sometimes include music that sounds a lot like Spanish music, along with the music our Quechua brothers in the Andes play. Some things do change."

Mariano rose from the stool where he had been sitting and went to stand behind his father. "A custom that hasn't changed is singing anents."

"I've heard about them," Art said. "Aren't they the songs that—as one of John's books says—make the world as we dream it?"

"Exactly." Mariano smiled at him. "Anents make things happen, turn our dreams into reality. They're a sort of magic. We continue to sing them, as well as our love songs."

There was a long silence as Rosa passed the chicha bowl. Then one of the women in our group pointed at two dogs playing outside the door. "I've heard that the dogs hunt with the men but belong to the women." She looked at Rosa. "Is that true?"

Rosa set down the chicha bowl and sat next to her husband. "Yes. We women take care of the dogs, training them and giving them ayahuasca when necessary. The dogs are essential for the men to use in the hunt because they're better hunters than men." She laughed loudly at this, and most of our group joined her. Mariano couldn't resist a smile, but he and his father refrained from laughing. "After all, men must rely on their eyes, while dogs use many senses very efficiently. They smell and hear the game, as well as see it. They even use their sense of taste, and they have the ability to dream their way into the trail of the animal they're tracking. But sometimes a dog may get lazy or cowardly. Then we prepare a special ayahuasca for him. The dog takes a dream journey that affects him deeply—and after that, almost always he becomes a good hunting dog. We women know how to do these things." She stood up and resumed straining the chicha, periodically scraping out pieces of yucca fiber with her finger and flicking them onto the floor.

"Won't that attract flies and roaches?" one of the women asked me, indicating the small pile of yucca fiber accumulating at Rosa's feet.

"They'll all be gone within the hour." I explained that jungle soils, including the hard-packed floors of the longhouse, are nutrient starved and that microorganisms immediately absorb things like the yucca fiber, converting them into substances that feed the forests. "You'll notice that if you vomit or have diarrhea when you take ayahuasca, all signs of it will be gone by morning. Nothing will remain—nothing at all!"

Tobacco

This last exchange about the role of microorganisms occurred in English; the Shuar were accustomed to my side conversations with members of our group, aware that I was often asked to explain things that did not require their input. When we stopped talking, Rosa spoke while wiping her hands on a large leaf. "When I was young"—her eyes moved around our circle—"about six years old, maybe, I started taking wild tobacco. My father gave me datura, but I didn't like it so much. I preferred the wild tobacco. My grandmother often took care of me, and she used to tell me that I could take as much as she could put in her hand. The tobacco is taken in a liquid form—we mix the dry leaves in water—and is sniffed slowly through the nose. This means you can't hold too much in the palm of your hand.

"My grandmother taught me how to prepare it at its very best. She used to say, 'Rosa, when you grow up you will be expected to take care of your family and home. I want to teach you to be an excellent wife and mother, so that your life will be full and happy. In order to have healthy children and grandchildren, you must prepare tobacco in the same way I do, in a medium-sized bowl. First, you pick the leaves and let them dry in the sun. After they're dry, roll them into something resembling a long stick (about one inch thick and eight inches long). Then, when you want to use the tobacco, slice off a section and let it dissolve in water.'"

One of the North American men asked, "Is this the same as the tobacco in cigarettes?"

The three Shuar laughed at this. Mariano replied. "Not at all. I've had plenty of your cigarettes, especially when I was in the army, fighting Peruvians. Our tobacco is a different animal—much stronger. Growing as it does in the jungle, it's full of arutam—though I will say that when you can't get Shuar tobacco, smoking cigarettes can work as a sort of substitute, particularly if you do it on an empty stomach. Remember, it's the spirit of the plant that counts, not the chemicals."

Rosa continued, "My grandmother had lots of arutam. Oh, she was powerful! When she gave me tobacco, she told me not to be afraid. 'If you fear it,' she said, 'its spirit is likely to kill you. But if you take it with courage, you'll have power. You'll be an arutam woman when you grow up. Only when you lose that power will you die. And if you take it at night, you will gain the power of the moon.' Then I fell asleep, and during my dreaming I received the power from the tobacco spirits."

The Role of the Teacher Plants

"Can you remember the first time you took ayahuasca?" Art asked Rosa.

"I remember it so well—like it was yesterday, but it wasn't yesterday. Oh, my, no. I was probably twelve years old. Whew! That long ago. . . . Well, my father had a little house, a special one for taking datura and ayahuasca, across the river from the strip where airplanes sometimes land, in the place we call Pankints. It was where my grandfather, who is now long gone into the other worlds, had lived in former days. In any case, my father brought lots of ayahuasca to that little house.

"We have to fast, as you know, before taking ayahuasca—this is very important. We neither eat nor sleep before or for a while after taking it. That plant, that spirit is an incredible teacher. It's the best of teachers! We must show it respect, because if we fail to do this, it can kill us. It's a teacher that really demands respect! When you take it, the earth trembles and everything changes. We shapeshift, we die, and then we're reborn. We transform and become new, emerging as the eagle or another animal with the great power of arutam. We've experienced death and have returned, so we know that death is nothing to fear. It's part of life and part of the continual transformation that occurs all the time between people and plants and animals, and the rivers and earth herself."

One of the men asked if any of the Shuar would comment on the relative importance of one plant as opposed to the others.

Rosa spoke up immediately. "For us Shuar the use of datura, tobacco, and ayahuasca has always been important. All three are essential to our lives. They are great teacher plants and spirits. Yet we must be very careful with them and treat them with the respect they require. We must measure the proper amounts—not too much, not too little. If we fail in this, they'll punish us. I've tried to teach all these things to my children and grandchildren, and I hope they'll teach them to theirs. You will, Mariano; I expect it of you and know you will—I've observed that you respect the old ways as well as some of the new ones.

"Older people—the elders, like me now—can give very important advice about the plants and the spirits. Can you believe it? I'm one of those wise old ones now! We know about dreams and about the journeys you take when you use the teacher plants. There are all kinds of dreams, some with snakes and some where awful things happen—scary dream journeys! Some of these tell the future. We elders usually can tell you about these dreams. We're knowledgeable in the ways of the spirits and in interpreting the dreams they bring to our people.

"We learn just about everything from the sacred teacher plants. That's where the real wisdom originates!"

Later that afternoon, as we sat in the lodge where the ayahuasca ceremony would soon begin, I listened to the participants chatting softly among themselves.

"What an honor," one of them said, "to be invited here to take ayahuasca with a Shuar shaman."

"I never would have believed people really live like this—that they hold such respect for the plants—if I hadn't experienced it myself."

Initiation into Adulthood

in the Words of

Mariano and Yaanua Patricia Arcos Tuitza

Mariano: I'm one of seven brothers and a sister who has died—shapeshifted to another place. As children we were considered innocent until six years of age, knowing only the names of our father and mother and siblings and some of the plants and animals. But at six everything changed.

That's when I was sent to primary school at the mission. My teacher taught us discipline and how to read and write. We knew nothing about education before this—and we all spoke with each other in the Shuar language. It wasn't until school that we learned Spanish. There the teachers taught us in both languages—Shuar and Spanish. That was most of what we studied that first year. In the second year we learned writing and arithmetic.

My friends and brothers and I always played together. Since I lived near the mission, I didn't have to go back home right after school; I could stay and play futbol (soccer). We also went down to the Rio Tsuirim and swam together sometimes. But our teachers constantly reminded us to behave. We learned to listen to their advice and the words of the priest: that it was important to be good children. We tried to obey them because if we were naughty, our father and mother punished us.

When we were still young our parents gave us ayahuasca—especially if we misbehaved. When we annoyed them or answered back, they turned us over to the teacher plants. Such was the discipline we received. That's how we were raised—and it's the same today.

When I turned eighteen, I was through with the pastimes of my childhood. That's when I entered the army—I've already told you about that. What I haven't mentioned, though, is our initiation into adulthood.

It happened like this. We were all at home with my father and mother, when our parents discussed plans to take us to the sacred waterfall. Long before dawn, we all left with my father—my brothers, our sister, and I. We started by taking tobacco so we might have the powers of our ancestors to see into the future and deal with the challenges that would confront us. It gives visions and takes us on journeys. We grind the leaves with water and then sniff the liquid through the nose, up both nostrils at the same time. Oh, it explodes the top off your head! Then you settle down. The initial jolt gives way to a shapeshift, as though you flow out through that hole in the top of your head and glide like a bat.

While we were flying with the spirit of the tobacco, our father said: "My children, tomorrow we'll hike to Tuntiak, the great rainbow who dwells in the heart of the sacred waterfall, so that you may have power, good fortune in your lives, and courage to face all obstacles like warriors. When you have spouses, you'll live well with them, taking care of them and your children. You'll always protect your families and honor your amikris."

We said: "Good, Papa. We're ready, we're eager."

Our mother harvested plantains and bananas so we'd have plenty of ripe ones. She presented them to us in a sort of ceremony and wished us well. We all knew that what was about to happen would change the way we looked at each other. We would transform from children to warriors, the same way that tadpoles shift into frogs.

The next day we set out for the sacred waterfall, trekking hard for eight hours. Then we rested, ate bananas and chicha, and traveled two more hours. The trail took us through dense jungle, not like the path up the river to the thermal waterfalls. It was rough, steep, and muddy. Finally we reached a beautiful grove, high above the river. We could hear the roar of the water—though we still were a good distance from the waterfall, we were close to the river. There on that knoll, with the river thundering below us, we built a lean-to of palm branches.

Since we were still children, we were hungry and thirsty, but our father wouldn't give us any food; when night came, we slept without eating.

In the morning we were starving—and dying of thirst! Or so we thought. We complained, but our father saw to it that we didn't eat or drink. He did prepare the tobacco, though, mixing it with saliva and water. We opened our hands. He poured some into each of our cupped palms and we sniffed it up our noses, accepting that powerful plant spirit and giving thanks.

Afterward, because it was still early, we set out again for the sacred waterfall. When we had almost arrived there and could hear the deafening roar of that mighty water, we stopped. We all looked around—at each other, at this magical place, at our father. We were overwhelmed with emotions, though we tried not to show it. We tried to be good warriors—our sister, too, a strong arutam woman— to concentrate on feeling the power and spirit of the tobacco.

We arranged ourselves in single file with our father in front. Then we walked forward, slowly, solemnly. When we were about twenty meters from the falls, he whistled and spoke to Tuntiak: "As an elder and their father, I have come to save my children and to give them power." Then he said to us: "Give me your hands."

We went forward together, as one, without looking up because we knew that you shouldn't raise your head to Tuntiak. We approached by wading in the shallow water near the edge of the deep pool—we'd been told that you must wait to bathe in the middle, where the falling water enters the pool.

Then my father spoke to the sacred waterfall. "Give my children strength," he said. "Give them arutam, the ferocity of the jaguar, the power of the anaconda." We felt what he said, respecting his words and desire. Our hearts were boiling with energy, like the ayahuasca when it bubbles over the fire. Our bodies shook.

There's a narrow rock ledge that leads under the sacred waterfall. The noise there is deafening, the force of the falling water equal to an avalanche. He motioned for us to walk along that ledge. Oh, what a moment! We struggled across the slippery rock and under the crashing water while it slammed us hard. Sometimes we couldn't bear it and fell, but we always managed to scramble back to our feet and stand there. We opened ourselves to Tsunkqui, allowing her power to crash into us, driving the arutam deep inside, into our hearts, filling us with the courage to face life and death as true Shuar, as adults. I'm telling you that it's not as easy as it sounds— receiving that type of energy!

Afterward, we turned around and walked slowly away, leaving Tuntiak, the sacred waterfall, and Tsunkqui behind us. Without looking back, we continued walking until nightfall. Finally, we came to a stopping place, where we took more tobacco. Our father said: "Accept this plant. Its spirit flows into you. Remember the times at home when you annoyed your mother while she was giving you yucca, those childish moments of fooling around. You must behave now. It's time you became adults." We fasted—eating no food, drinking no chicha so that the tobacco took effect—and each of us, with the help of our father, lay down and began to journey. While we journeyed in the trance, we received the power of arutam.

For me, the message was to be a warrior, to face all enemies with courage—and also to be full of love, a good father who is able to take care of my children and my wife. My power is very beautiful to me; it makes me brave in fighting. This is the strength that the anaconda has given me. At midnight I was dizzy from the tobacco— as if I were drunk, but totally aware, as in a dream.

Besides receiving our own arutam, we also journeyed to each other's deaths. We saw where we would go, how we would shapeshift out of this human life. I can personally attest to the incredible power of these journeys. As my amikri knows, years later, when our sister died giving birth to her tenth child, we all understood where she was going. We'd seen it. We were sad to lose her and heartbroken for her children—especially the new baby who would never know his mother—but we were comforted because we knew that she was shifting into a beautiful place.

In the morning we all felt good. It had been a magical time for each of us. We were arutam Shuar. Our father gave us plantains for breakfast, ground up into powder—only half a pinch. If you take more than that small amount, you can really lose it, going on dark journeys, almost as though you are dying.

The next day we made our way through the forest back to our home. Our mother was waiting there to greet us. Yet we knew that in a certain sense, the journey into initiation had only begun. She gave us each four portions of ayahuasca. We were embraced by this plant, engulfed by the realities of its world. While shapeshifting with the ayahuasca, we hiked up into the mountains until we arrived at a special place where a huge tree grows, taller even than all the enormous giants surrounding it. It's a grandfather tree, older than time itself. Beneath it we built a lean-to, gathered dry wood, and lit a fire. Our father prepared more ayahuasca and set it over the fire to brew.

We climbed into the top of that ancient tree and erected a platform. We hoisted a tunduli, a hollow-log drum that can be heard for miles, up to the platform.

Then we returned to the ground just as the dark night closed in. We sat around the fire while our father told a few stories. Eventually we fell asleep under the stars, the ayahuasca boiling next to us.

The tunduli woke us the next morning. It was still dark. Our father had climbed up to the platform and was playing that drum. "Tun–du, tun–du, tun–du." It echoed throughout the forests, helping the plants and animals greet the new day, welcoming in the spirits of the rivers, rocks, and mountains. It would continue all day, the beating of the drum. We took turns playing it, climbing to the top of the tree to beat out the rhythm. We knew others might hear it and come to join us. Ernesto Chumpi, son of the great shaman, arrived in our clearing late in the afternoon. He told us he'd heard the drum and wanted to honor us.

All day long we brewed the ayahuasca. We needed plenty! It was our initiation, and we are a big family. As the sun was setting, we started dividing it up. We arranged a total of thirty bowls around the area near the giant tree. The ceremony began when my father said: "Accept these offerings from the plants, from Ayumpum. Drink down these bowls so that you will know the great power of life."

After we drank the ayahuasca, there was a great deal of vomiting. It sounded like a place where hundreds of volcanoes were erupting!

We were cleaning out all the remaining jealousies and weaknesses of childhood, making ourselves pure so we could completely accept the arutam and our responsibilities as adults to take care of future generations. In my journey, a powerful presence came to me. "I am here for you," it said in a voice deeper than thunder. "I am the jaguar; I am the anaconda." I became one with that voice, the presence, and one with millions of sounds and forms. I shapeshifted into stones, trees, the jaguar. I saw that I'm arutam, so powerful that no one can conquer me. With all my strength no one can win over me. I have the arutam essential for the warrior. I also saw that we must protect future generations—but not just our human children. I saw the warrior as the guardian of all generations of trees, birds, animals, fishes, insects, rocks, and rivers. That's the arutam of the warrior. It's my dream to fulfill.

Oh, how that time together empowered each of us! What we learned from those plants! We saw so much about ourselves and each other. We came to understand the realities of the forest, of what it is to be human. Above all, for me, I learned this: In order to gain arutam, to live a happy life, you must take the necessary journeys. You have to be brave to have the powers of ayahuasca, tobacco, and datura—the three most important teachers. You have to face your fears and conquer them.

I want to add that on my journeys I've never been asked to kill someone; that's not the point, not the way to use arutam. I've been told to be brave and have been shown that I have great strength, power that I must use to protect my children and their children and the children of the forests. It's up to me to do the rest. I'm an adult Shuar. I must take responsibility for what needs to be done to defend the things we love.

Each of us received our messages, our lessons and missions. The initiation was an incredible experience, a shapeshift that altered each of us forever. We grew strong overnight, and we bonded as never before—with each other, with nature, with the world. We also learned then that an initiation is not an ending; it's the beginning. During those days when we became adults, we entered portals that took us into new realities. We saw what our lives are about, who we are, where we've been, and where we must go.

When you want to have powerful journeys like the ones we had, it's important to not eat or drink anything. This opens you up. Then, during the journey, you may become a jaguar. Or you may stand there alone and see a jaguar with a stone in her mouth. When this happens, you have to rush forward, grab the stone, and remove it from her mouth. A jaguar you see might open its mouth, bare its teeth, and make horrible noises. You must run up to it and touch it; it will give you power and energy.

Everyone is afraid of jaguars. They're warrior animals with blood-curdling growls and screams. And the anaconda is just as fierce and frightening. All people fear them. Overcoming these fears is the way to arutam. Never shrink from these things. Shapeshift into them or into someone who's strong enough to touch them. Accept the gifts they offer. If we summon the courage and faith to take the power of arutam from these animals, we become kakaram men.

Women can also seize the power of arutam. When they drink ayahuasca, tobacco, and datura, they journey like men. I know from my mother, sister, and wife that arutam is what gives them the power to be great mothers and wives. It teaches them to shapeshift with the plants and train the dogs, to work with Nunqui, and to protect themselves from the deadly snakes that live near the yucca gardens. It also teaches them to make the sweetest chicha. And the wild tobacco? Arutam women make the finest. Nunqui helps them nurture the seedlings, pamper the plants, and dry the leaves. Many men want to marry the woman who knows how to grow and prepare fine tobacco!

All of this comes out of our initiations. I'll do the same for my children as my father did for me. I want them to learn the power of the teacher plants and of that mighty rainbow, Tuntiak, of trekking through the jungle while flying high with the spirit of tobacco. I want them to meet the jaguar and anaconda, see their deaths, feel the thundering sacred waterfalls, understand their dream of life, commit themselves to their missions.

Yaanua ("Star Woman") Patricia Arcos Tuitza: The initiation
ceremony for women is very similar to the one for men. My parents
introduced me to ayahuasca when I was eight years old. There were
about fifteen of us—all girls—and we took it together. My mother,
a great herbal healer and shaman, prepared the plant for us.

The tunduli played out its rhythm the entire time. We girls took
many bowls of ayahuasca. Oh, so much! Then we vomited and
vomited—we really cleaned ourselves out, opening ourselves to the
power of the forests, arutam. The sound of us all purging was
amazing; I still remember it as though it were yesterday: huaaak,
huaaak, huaaak! My recollection is vivid, and yet it happened nearly
thirty years ago!

My journey was incredible. I began to see my own future. In those
days, I never thought I would leave the jungle; I didn't want to. I
loved it here so much. But the ayahuasca showed me the truth. I saw
mountains, higher than the Cutucú, covered in snow. They were great
mountains—not just the Andes, but other mountains, too, far away.
I dreamed of a man who was extremely tall and pale. He wore a
strange hat. At his side was a grown woman who looked a little like
me. They were a couple with children. They smiled at me and seemed
happy, ecstatic. I saw them wandering from the mountains back to
the jungle.

Of course, later I came to understand this dream. I did leave the
jungle, journeying up into the Andes to study at a university in Quito.
Then I went to Europe, to the Alps, and married a tall man from
Austria. His name is Helmut. He was wearing that funny hat when I
met him, just like in the ayahuasca vision. We have three wonderful
children now. Nantar is twelve. She's named after a red amulet, a
stone we sometimes find in the banana orchards that comes from a
bird's gullet, and brings luck. Amaru is seven. His name means
"spirit of the anaconda," the most powerful force in the forest.
Yancua is only a year old, named after the brightest star in the sky.
We see that star early in the evening, and it's the last one in the sky
as Etsaa rises.

When Helmut asked where I wanted to live, I said, "In the

jungle." I'm like most Shuar in this regard. We may travel away from here, explore other parts of the world, but we always return. There's no better place, no better life—not anywhere. It may get hot here sometimes, and we do have bugs and snakes. But overall, there's nothing like it! If you compare our problems with those in the big cities, we don't really have any problems here—absolutely nothing to complain about! Although Helmut is a very social person, he agreed. He said to me "Okay; let's try it." He loves it here, too. It's a great place to raise our children.

The ayahuasca journey of my initiation told me many other things, too. I really understood the power of the forests and the importance they have in our lives. No matter where we live—even for those people in the Alps—these trees and animals here bring us power and luck. They help to balance the world. I saw this back when I was eight and I have come to understand it even better over the years. If the forests are destroyed, we'll all die with them.

The Shaman
and Dream Change

My work with the Shuar led me to other indigenous peoples of South America, including Ipupiara, a member of the Ureu-eu-wau-wau, a tribe in the Brazilian rain forests. Like so many before them, the Ureu-eu-wau-wau are the victims of modern society's avaricious demands for lumber, gold, and cattle—their numbers have been decimated during my lifetime from four thousand to today's forty-two. Ipupiara and I became close friends, and he invited me to participate in a traditional ceremony that made us blood brothers.

After a long shamanic apprenticeship with his tribal elders, Ipupiara had been encouraged by the Ureu-eu-wau-wau to attend school to learn the ways of the "developed" world. Eventually he earned a Ph.D. in anthropology and biology from a Brazilian university and became fluent in Portuguese, Spanish, and English, as well as eight indigenous dialects. He and his wife, Cleicha—who was Quechua, a native of the Peruvian Andes, and a highly respected shamanic healer in her own right—joined me in workshops around the United States and were instrumental, along with Shuar uwishin and shamans from the Andes, in establishing Dream Change Coalition.* In 1997 the Ureu-eu-

*For more information on the Ureu-eu-wau-wau, the amazing story of Ipupiara and Cleicha, the circumstances of our meeting, and the creation of Dream Change Coalition, see *Shapeshifting,* (Rochester, Vt.:Destiny Books, 1997), pp. 156–61.

wau-wau bestowed upon Ipupiara the title of Makunaiman, "the one who makes things possible."

This title is reserved for master shamans who have left the security of the tribe in order to teach others and then return to take their place in the Sacred Council of Elders.

Late one afternoon I had a telephone conversation with Ipupiara that would—entirely unbeknownst to me at the time—figure significantly in the creation of this book, as well as confirm for me once more the power of arutam, shamanic journeying, and those who have shapeshifted out of this life.

"I must tell you about this dream I had." I could clearly hear Ipupiara's smile in his voice. "I was journeying—you know, just letting go, asking the spirits to take me wherever I needed to be. Suddenly my vision was clouded, and something fuzzy appeared in front of me, moving and flapping its wings. Guess what it was."

"A bat?"

"Yes—how did you know? But then I knew you would. I knew that somehow this was all connected to you."

"Go on. What happened next?"

"It flew away. I followed. It led me to a waterfall—very high, with a great rainbow cutting through it."

"Tuntiak."

"What?"

"Sacred waterfall of the Shuar," I explained, "where initiations are held, where the first man and woman were created—according to ancient mythology."

Ipupiara was silent for a moment. "How incredible! I was there, John. I followed that bat right into the waterfall, and then I saw an old man standing beneath the falls, the water pounding down on him. He held a bowed instrument to his mouth—you know, one of those we play like a mouth harp."

"It was Chumpi."

"Who?"

I realized that I had never mentioned Chumpi to Ipupiara, nor had I told him of the shaman's shapeshift into a bat. I did so now, briefly relating the events leading up to it and my final contact with the great uwishin. "He had predicted it, told me it would happen. . . . He has never returned in human form. No one has seen him as a man since just before that evening when he failed to show up for our ceremony and the bat came instead. Now the bat returns every time we hold ceremonies in Miazal. It's been four years since his shapeshift, and still the bat always flies in to join us."

Once again there was silence on the other end of the phone, except for the sound of breathing. "Isn't life amazing?" Ipupiara asked at last. "There he was, beneath that cascade, absorbing all that energy, the arutam of the falls. The bat took me there. . . . Chumpi is the bat, the bat is Chumpi. He comes to you whenever you're there physically. He came to me just a short while ago."

"What did he say to you?"

"He smiled and told me he was glad that you and I had finally met. He said to always encourage you to keep following your path; you know the way, but sometimes you forget—or think you do. He said I should be with you like a big brother, guiding you, coaxing you along. . . . And he said something else. . . . That we should make sure to let the shamans speak."

I nodded on my end of the phone. "Of course—it's important."

"And he said this: We should listen to the voices of the old ones, those who have shapeshifted out of this life—like him. The spirits of the ones we call 'dead' are powerful, arutam spirits. Each of us needs to hear them out. They'll liberate us, showing us that life is a dream, breaking the vines that tie us to the ground, freeing us to fly. He cautioned us not to leave the job of this listening to anyone else—not even to shamans. We each must take on this wonderful task. We all have ancestors who have shapeshifted, and we need to contact them, sit before them in a circle, and open our hearts to their wisdom."

It was quite some time after this phone conversation that Ehud and I put together the idea for this book. When Ipupiara learned that Mariano would be taping the stories of Shuar uwishin, he was ecstatic. We were sitting together, sipping beer in the lobby of a San Francisco hotel, waiting to begin a workshop. "Perhaps we can make a book of the Ureu-eu-wau-wau next," he said. He paused then, lost in thought. "But I'm not sure there are enough of us left—enough of the wise elders whose tapes could fill a book." He sat quietly for a while. Then he grinned suddenly, as if something had just occurred to him. "Of course!" He raised the beer in a toast. "*That's* what Chumpi meant about letting the shamans speak: your amikri must get their stories onto the tapes for your book."

I suddenly realized how right Ipupiara was. I clinked my glass against his. "It makes perfect sense!"

Together we came up with the idea of asking a few of the Shuar shamans—men and women, old and young—to exchange their stories. Mariano agreed to take on the assignment of recording their conversations. This was relatively easy, since most of them were the uwishin he had been interviewing all along. He simply focused on their shamanism, encouraging them to discuss healings they had done, initiations, their personal shapeshifts, and their relationships with the DCC groups. We also decided to include conversations I had had with some of them. In making these tapes and recording the shamans' words here, in writing, we have followed the instructions of Chumpi and listened to his voice, that of an old one who has shapeshifted out of this life. He told us to let the shamans speak. What follows comes directly from them.

Shamanic Healing

Amalia Tuitza

"You want me to talk about healing the gringos? Well, I can tell you a thing or two. Let's begin with something that happened just a few days ago. John brought a gringo to me who had been stung by a scorpion. That silly foreigner got up in the morning and grabbed his shirt from where he'd left it lying in a heap in his chair—foolish, foolish man. Grandpa scorpion was just waiting there, probably sleeping and scared near to death when that huge white hand reached in and started shaking everything in sight. So—whammo—he struck!

"That's right. He struck that gringo right on the thumb. Ouch! I saw the look on this man's face, and so I asked him what he felt about the scorpion. Of course, I myself didn't ask him because he couldn't understand a word I said in either Shuar or Spanish. I told John to ask.

"'Felt?' he said. 'About the scorpion?' At first, he peered at me like I was crazy. Then that man started to laugh—oh, how much that told me! He said he never expected a question like that, but now that he thought about it, he felt that the scorpion was testing him, giving him a warning. He told John that he didn't think the scorpion had any evil intent.

"'Then you'll be fine,' I assured him. 'No need for anything special here; no plant spirit is required.' I put some *trago* [locally brewed alcohol] in a bowl and told him to keep his thumb in it for a little while. That was just to take away some of the pain and make him forget about everything. I said, 'Drink some of that trago, too!' I wanted him to journey into the spirit of the scorpion. It could give him some arutam.

"He came back to me a little later and asked if I thought it would be all right for him to join the rest of the group on the hike up the cliffs to the thermal waterfall. I looked him over. He seemed in excellent spirits. His energy was way up. I told him it was a beautiful day for a hike. 'Go on,' I encouraged him. 'Just watch out where you stick that thumb!'

"You know, we have a saying that the world is as you dream it. If that man had dreamed a dream that made the scorpion angry or even if he'd just believed that the scorpion had it in for him, he could have been taken very ill—even died. But he was a smart man. He was open to accepting a little arutam.

"That was a healing. I didn't do anything. It was a gift from the scorpion.

"Another time John brought a woman who had sprained her ankle. It swelled to the size of a coconut. Oh, she was in a fix! You could smell her fear. She was convinced it was broken. I had to change that dream for her. I told her that datura could heal even a broken bone and heal it overnight. When she heard the word *datura* she took another fright and shook her head violently, like a dog with a lizard in her mouth. 'No!' she shouted. I had to laugh. I figured she'd heard stories about people taking datura through their mouths, about our initiation ceremonies, the shamanic journeys that last a week or so.

"'Oh, no,' I told her. 'What you're thinking of is not what I had in mind.' I assured her that datura—on the skin outside, not consumed—is a powerful medicine, a healer, but without the deep dreaming states. Perfectly safe—when you know what you're doing, as my mother who taught me did, and as I do. We made a poultice of the datura leaves and wrapped it in a cloth around her ankle.

Next day she was up and walking!

I didn't bother to explain that it's the same spirit whether you take it in your belly or around your ankle. Datura—what a wonderful friend and spirit! I did nothing, as usual; the plant is the doctor."

Bosco Tuitza

"I'm Amalia's brother. You've heard what she's told you about the ways she helps people, including gringos. I can tell you another story. I'm a shaman, and I know how these things work. This one is about the man who started us on this path with the foreigners—your amikri John, Mariano.

"John fell off the cliff near the river and broke his knee. You should have seen it! All bloody and swollen and awful. His group of people had left that morning—flown away on the plane for the Andes. John let down his guard. He was preparing for a long trek through the forest to go and visit other Shuar friends and was trying to relax after guiding all those people for such a long time. He'd been teaching them and working very hard, so he took some time to rest before his journey; he was swimming at the river, climbing out of the water to head up that cliff where we dive, when he fell.

"Amalia gave him datura to put on his knee. She taught her daughter, Yajanua Maria, how to prepare it, cutting and mashing and mixing it just right, and then tying it around his knee with a leaf and vine, or a bandana, if they had one. Maria accompanied him on the trek to his other Shuar friends. Every morning and night she fixed the datura for him and took care of him. They went farther into the forest, to places I've never seen. John walked like a jaguar. Who would have known that just a few days earlier he had fallen off a cliff and broken his knee? That's how my sister, doña Amalia, works.

"I too am a shaman, but I work mainly with ayahuasca, helping people move into the world of the spirits and change their dreams."

Rosa Shakai

"Many injuries are healed with plants—by using them on the skin like poultices. This is what Amalia excels at. Much of this work is done by women shamans. We grandmothers teach our daughters.

"But sometimes things need to be treated by the ayahuasca shamans like Bosco Tuitza, through journeys deep into the world of the spirits. Every family does this, and we all have these kinds of shamans. Our families often take ayahuasca in milder doses than those used in the healing ceremonies. We sit together and share our experiences.

"However, there are certain uwishin who are known to be especially skilled in working with the ayahuasca spirits. When the family shamans have not been able to help the person in need, we go to one of these. Everyone knows who the best ones are. Mostly they're men these days, although in the past there were also women who did this. Why aren't there more women doing this anymore? I'm not sure. There are no women priests in the missions either. . . . Do you think that has anything to do with it?"

Tuntuam

"Juan Gabriel is another from the outside world who trusts our medicine. He came all the way out here after he was in a bad automobile accident up in the Andes. The driver was killed. They rushed Juan Gabriel to the hospital, thinking he was going to die. But guess what? He left the hospital and took a bus to Shell. Then he got a ride in on the mission plane and came to see me.

"He was in a lot of pain, and there was a bone sticking out of his chest! I gave him ayahuasca—we took it together. Juan Gabriel is like my son—I had to help him, together with the ayahuasca; we had to heal him. And we did. The spirit of the ayahuasca, the *tsentsak,* did all the work. He didn't die. He learned something, too, from all that. Now he's like new. He even climbs mountains again, up into the glaciers of the great volcanoes!

"This tells you something about the power of ayahuasca, tsentsak, arutam."

Daniel Wachapa

"Ayahuasca is an arutam spirit. You might say it's the canoe that carries arutam. Whooosh!—it glides down the river and into our souls . . . shapeshifting, transforming us.

"I'm very careful to honor its spirit when I cut the vine and prepare it. There's no secret to how this is done. John can show you the method; he knows it well. The important thing is the spirit of the plant, loving it, respecting it, feeling its strength. After cleaning and slicing the vine and placing it gently in the pot, we count out twenty-five leaves from one of the other plants—usually yage—and lay them on top of the ayahuasca. In the old days the Shuar could only count to five; we didn't need higher numbers. We uwishin still use the method of our fathers: We count out five leaves and hold them between our thumb and first finger; then five more and put them between the first and second fingers. In this way we get to twenty. Then we hold the last five in our other hand. At that point we know we have the right number.

"The patient lies in front of me on the bench. I shapeshift into a volcano or anaconda full of arutam! I bring up the tsentsak—the invisible darts that were planted in my heart by my teacher—and I blow them inside the body in front of me. Through them I can look into the patient, seeing clearly the work I must do. The tsentsak tell me everything: where the problem originated and what to do to remove it. I suck on the patient, I the anaconda, pulling the terrible energy out of my patient and into me. The volcano burns it, destroys it, freeing the patient—and me—from the pains, the illness, whatever the problem was.

"We cure all types of diseases in this way. The Shuar have done this since the time when we were created, when the first man and woman leaped out of Tuntiak, the rainbow in the sacred waterfall, springing to life simultaneously, not separately, as the Bible tells of the creation of man and woman. Ayumpum, Etsaa's brother, the god of lightning, brought us the knowledge. Tsunkqui, the water goddess, was the first to use it, the first shaman. She rode the giant turtle, and that's the reason we shamans often sit on turtle stools—and why for certain problems we prefer Tsunkqui ayahuasca, the type that grows along the rivers. That great vine is the child of the anaconda, created when Amaru [spirit of the anaconda] dances with Tsunkqui.

"With our own people, I've cured all the diseases caused by bad energy, envy, and evil spirits: influenza, broken bones, soul loss, gripe, headaches, sicknesses in the stomach, infertility, infections, impotence—all those sorts of things. I've cured many similar ailments among the gringos, and also problems we aren't accustomed to here, like tension, cancer, and what they call chronic fatigue.

"John came to me one time with a terrible infection in his leg. He said the doctors in his country told him they might have to amputate it. They put him in the hospital, but he left and came here. I saw the vengeful spirit in it and sucked it out. The next morning he was better. Within a few days, the infection was gone.

"One time, John and Eve Bruce, a medical doctor from the United States and a good friend of mine, introduced me to a deaf woman. With the ayahuasca I was able to see the cause of her loss, that when she was younger she'd wished she didn't have to hear those around her. She'd even dreamed of it. We went on a journey together, she and I, and understood that as a girl things had been said in her family that were too painful for her to hear. But now that was different; she was a grown woman and could change that dream. So we did it—and she recovered her hearing. John told me that later all of her balance returned, something she'd lost when her hearing went away.*

"I've also been to the United States with Eve and John. They took me, along with other shamans from South America, to speak to and heal people in California, Michigan, and New York. Over two thousand people came to our conferences. I'd never seen so many! We also met with over two hundred experts at a medical school there. I used the same methods as I do here and cured many of their people, even those with serious problems, including depression, broken hearts, cancers, dysfunctional digestive systems . . . so many things. Eve is an incredible person, a highly respected doctor, a surgeon who understands how to operate on people using a knife, and also one who is open to our work, who studies it seriously and understands the spirit of the Shuar, the power of tsentsak and arutam. She's a very good friend. She's seen that we can operate without using the knife! We've taught each other many things."

Shamanic Training and Initiation

Bosco Tuitza

"You asked to hear the story of how I became a shaman. That's what you want to learn about, right? Well, I'll tell it to you.

"Long ago, maybe sixty or seventy years, when I was a very young man, before I reached puberty, my uncle was a shaman. He'd been told by his guides that he would be killed, so he called me to him and said that he wanted to pass on his knowledge and powers to me—even though I hadn't yet made love to my first woman.

"My uncle gave me a clear liquid to drink; it contained tsentsak, the invisible darts shamans use to transform things and to cure illness. He told me not to speak a word or eat a thing for three days. On the fourth I could

*See chapter 5, footnote, page 97.

drink some chicha. It was a difficult period for me. Training to do this work isn't easy! Our bodies try to reject the tsentsak. My uncle put me through a tough initiation. I couldn't have sex for a year—but since I was so young, that didn't really matter to me. After many months, my strength grew. I learned to use the tsentsak; they accepted me and my body accepted them. I became a powerful shaman.

"As my uncle had predicted, he was killed—in a battle. As soon as it happened, I felt his arutam enter me like lightning. I became even more powerful! Now I'm able to use these powers not only to help my own people but also to work with and teach the white people, to help them heal and change their lives. I give them ayahuasca; I take them on journeys; and I use the tsentsak to remove the bad things I see inside them, the illnesses and other problems, the harmful spirits and the envy that's sent to them by others.

"I travel a long way to visit John and his groups, from my home far down the river. It takes me at least three days of walking very rapidly to get here—sometimes longer if it's rained and the rivers are swollen. But I do it because the gringos need me—they need the ayahuasca and the visions it brings, and they need the healings I can give them. On occasions when I am here in Miazal, I build a raft from wood and return home on it, going with the current of the river. But it's tricky business, very risky and full of too many adventures. When I was young—phew! Who cared! But now, I'm more serious. I have plenty of adventures on ayahuasca and when I heal people. I can live without the ones on the river. I'll live better, perhaps. Certainly longer!"

Antonio Charapa

"Although in my youth time wasn't important, and I don't know for sure my own age, I think I'm approximately eighty-five years old. And my wife is about the same.

"I first married a girl from another community, outside our province. I had two children with her. One is still alive, but the other died as an infant. After the child died, my wife left me. I was alone. I thought about becoming a shaman, especially when many members of my family—grandparents, uncles, aunts, and cousins—were becoming very sick and dying. I also knew that in the past my ancestors were powerful shamans.

"I discussed the matter with a man who was himself a shaman, and he told me that a black shaman had stolen my energy. Maybe, I thought, I could protect myself and save others by becoming a shaman. So I studied long and hard and became one, and now I'm able to live as a happily married man. My second wife's name is Teresa Tiris, and she and I have three daughters.

"The other wife died after suffering for almost eight years. Not even a shaman could save her. He made sacrifices to cure her, but he wasn't successful. Sometimes we simply must shapeshift out of this life. There's nothing a shaman can do to change this.

"I now live with a daughter in the center of Guyamar, near Miazal. I'm still a shaman—I continue to heal people and help them shapeshift with ayahuasca. I cure people who are sick. I know that I'm the best of five shamans who were part of my circle. We were all friends, and all of them worked together to give me the power to become a better shaman.

Tuntuam

"For me, it happened late in life. I was married, with children when I became deathly ill. Oh, I thought I would die! I wanted to; I would have welcomed a new form, a different body, a new beginning. But no, that wasn't my fate.

"So an old shaman found me and said he could cure me—which he did! What an amazing relief. I'd been with shamans all my life, seen their miracles. But this—it was something else! He used ayahuasca and tsentsak and brought in so many powerful spirits.

"After that, he said the only reason it worked, the only reason I was cured, was so that I myself could become a shaman and help others. He told me I had a journey to take before I could finally shapeshift, that I would suffer, but should always keep my faith, that I was here to do things, to heal people—and also help those from far away, over the Cutucú, to learn about us, about arutam and the forests.

"He put me through quite a training! I expected it to be difficult but not that tough! My body didn't like those tsentsak—not at the beginning. I had to fast and give up sex for a very long time—fasting for days and no sex for about a year! I had to avoid getting my head wet in the rivers. How tough is that for a Tsunkqui man?

"Why do we have to forego all those things? Because they're so powerful that they might interfere with the tsentsak. When the invisible darts are first placed in your heart, they're like a new plant, a little weak. Of course, over time they grow strong. But for that initial period, they need to be nurtured and protected. We Shuar know the powers of the rivers and certain foods. We understand that sex—orgasm—is like ayahuasca; it takes us into other worlds and shows us our connection with nature. That feeling, those waves deep inside, the fire—we unite with all the elements. The power of sex and of rivers and foods can hurt the tender tsentsak. We have to be very careful. If we do it right, the tsentsak show their appreciation by growing and returning the favor. They give us the power to see inside our patients and heal them.

"Training is never over. Sometimes the shaman must undergo horrible ordeals. Do you know how I was crippled? It happened while I was healing one of the gringo women. I was struck down. What a terrible moment! Everything left me; I saw nothing. For how long, I don't know. When I came to my senses, my family was circled around me. John was trying to talk to me, and so was Juan Gabriel. I couldn't hear them. One half of my body has been paralyzed ever since. But I've worked to heal myself, and now I'm much better. I can even walk, with a staff to help me.

"The woman was healed—that's what Juan Gabriel and John tell me. But they were so concerned about me. They asked if they should stop bringing groups here. I said, 'What for? Of course not. What happened to me is a sign that we're winning. Your people must come, they must learn from us. That's my mission. I can't rest until I've helped save these forests and my people by teaching and healing yours.'

"You know that if an enemy thinks you're weak, he doesn't worry about you. If he sees you as strong, he prepares hard and attacks you first. That's how it is. I know that John and the people he brings are doing important things—teaching their people about the need to change. We are winning. That means resistance will come, that the enemies will attack us. We can't give in to that. It's a sign that now is the time to fight harder.

"All this is part of my training. For the shaman it never ends. The more we experience, the harder the battle, the better we get. Initiation is the beginning."

Yajanua Maria Arcos

"My mother told me that the only good way to learn about the plants is to develop a close relationship with them, so she introduced me to ayahuasca at an early age. I learned fast. I was able to see things and understand them better.

"Then one day, when I was a young woman, she said it was time for me to get better acquainted with datura. Boy, that scared me! I studied medicine at the university in Quito and know the things they say about that plant. They say it makes you crazy. We Shuar know that it can kill, too. But my mother is powerful. How could I refuse her? I took her datura. Oh, what a nightmare! The first three days were a journey into blackness. I was out flat in bed, totally immobilized. I thought I was done for. Then my mother said it was time for more! Can you believe it?

"She gave me another dose. Wow! It changed everything. I saw my ancestors. I understood what I'd heard all my life, that our ancestors become powerful animals and live in the waterfalls, that they bring us arutam. We just have to accept them, open our hands to their gifts. I also saw the coming of white people to our lands, many foreigners who need to open their hearts, to understand things that reach way beyond the subjects taught in their schools.

"I did learn about datura, and I haven't taken it since—no need; I learned what I needed to from that plant. I talk with it, using it to heal bruises and other injuries. Sometimes, though, like most Shuar, I take ayahuasca.

"That datura my mother gave me helped me integrate my medical training with the wisdom of the shamans, the uwishin. What an initiation!"

Dream Change

The discussions with the shamans went beyond their personal healing work, shapeshifts, and initiations. They also sent very strong messages that we—the outsiders who come to learn from them—need to change our ways. The idea frequently repeated was that the world is as you dream it, that if you don't like things the way they are, then you must change the dream.

After DCC had been established, we struggled with how to structure ourselves. We knew that we did not want to be another pyramidal organization, reflecting the patriarchal structures that have dominated for the past several centuries. We visualized instead the creation of something new, an organization that was fluid and would allow people from all spectrums of life to follow their dreams. Rather than identifying jobs and then searching for men and women whose resumes told us they had excelled in these areas before, we felt we would be more effective if people created their own jobs that responded to their personal dreams and then took responsibility for ensuring their own success. We also embraced the idea that the new organization would—like the Shuar and other indigenous communities—balance the male and female, providing a forum for the feminine aspects of each of us to say "no" to the masculine propensity to cut more trees, build larger houses, and destroy what we all love in the name of progress.

The shamans pointed out that this "new" form was, in fact, very old. It is the way the Shuar—and most other cultures around the world—have managed themselves for nearly all of human history, during times when the earth's resources were well protected and vast. It has only been in the recent past, a mere blip on the screen of time, that it has been otherwise; throughout this brief period humans have squandered and mismanaged those resources and driven millions of species into extinction.

The shamans enthusiastically assured us that our dream for a nonhierarchical, balanced, and sustainable structure could easily manifest. "It's the way we've always functioned," Chumpi told us before shapeshifting out of his human form. "If I declare war on an enemy, I ask other men to join me, but the decision is theirs. Taking the warpath must be part of their dream as well as mine. And after the raid, those warriors who followed me return to their families. They're no longer under my command; they can do as they please. I'm the war chief for only a short period of time. The Shuar have never had tribal leaders—just people who take responsibility for specific jobs."

"When we face a crisis," Tuntuam added, "we sit in a circle, drink chicha, and work it out. Someone steps forward as the leader to help us move through that crisis. He forms his own circle, they take action, then it's over."

I recalled that during the ten years when I served as a consultant to the World Bank and United Nations—the decade after leaving the Peace Corps and prior to forming Independent Power Systems—I witnessed these types of fluid organizations within cultures around the world. I saw them at work among the Bugis on the island of Sulawesi in Indonesia, the Bedouin in the deserts of Iran, the Aborigines of Australia—and had read that it was the same for the Iroquois and Abenaki in my own native land of North America.

Daniel Wachapa summed it up succinctly. "You can dig a hole," he told us, "drop the seed in, cover it with earth, protect it from foraging animals, but in the end it is up to the great spirits and the plant whether it wants to become full grown or not."

Peem suggested that, as a complement to DCC, we help the Shuar create an organization that would be recognized by the outside world. He volunteered to take on the job of materializing that dream in Ecuador. Norma Asencio offered to be his North American counterpart. Norma was born and raised in Colombia and eventually became a U.S. citizen and licensed psychotherapist who focused on helping Hispanic families. After volunteering to assist DCC with a Christmas mailing, she eventually devoted more and more time to our work—until she found herself on the DCC payroll. Norma saw that DCC's Pollution Offset Lease for Earth (POLE) program would be a perfect partner for Peem's emerging foundation, which the Shuar had decided to name after the god of enlightenment, Ayumpum.

POLE grew out of the need among industrialized countries to mitigate against poisonous greenhouse gases (primarily CO_2). It is also intended to change the belief that the economic benefit of forests is the value resulting when they are cut for timber, cattle pastures, urban development, or oil, gold, and mineral exploitation. This new model begins with the premise that standing trees provide us with a highly valuable asset, a mechanism for cleaning up the pollution our industries and cars pour into the atmosphere. Buying a POLE becomes a means for including standing trees as a commodity in the market-based world economies. When individuals or corporations purchase a POLE, they lease rain forests that absorb greenhouse gases.

Besides leasing forests, POLE money is used to finance educational programs directed at increasing the awareness of what must be done in order to live in sustainable ways and ensure that future generations will prosper. POLE recognizes that preservation is not sufficient; the process must also include "changing the dream."

The Ayumpum Foundation integrated POLE into the Shuar culture. "Who knows forest stewardship better than we do?" Peem asked. "Traditionally, we only cut trees out of necessity. Today it has become about the only way to earn cash. POLE can change all that by paying us to keep the forests standing."

DCC has been careful to ensure that land ownership remains with the Shuar. POLE payments are for year-long leases only. This policy serves a dual purpose: it allows the Shuar to retain their property rights, and it keeps the whole program competitive on a market basis. Although this may run counter to conventional thinking among many conservationists—who prefer "in perpetuity" arrangements—it seems like the only just way to conduct a partnership and honor the true long-term economic worth of this valuable asset.

In addition to paying the individual families for protecting—rather than cutting—their forests, the Ayumpum Foundation takes uwishin-inspired teachings into the mission schools, promoting shamanism, songs, dances, and other customs that honor the traditional, nature-based ways of living. The idea that reading, writing, and arithmetic can replace the old knowledge is being supplanted by a recognition that the two complement each other."

Something similar to the Shuar's Ayumpum Foundation was taking root at the same time in the United States. The World Dream Institute was formed specifically to introduce the spirit of the Shuar to "Northern" schoolchildren. Teachers found that Shuar stories, music, and art helped students understand the relationships between people and nature; they also provided ways for children to help each other work through personal problems, overcoming tendencies toward depression and violence. As an added benefit, when classes combined such skills with writing and distributing books (to parents, local businesses, and libraries), the end result included higher test scores in reading, writing, art, and mathematics. The World Dream Institute had started as an experimental program, but quickly expanded to include a growing number of public and private schools throughout the United States.

Together the uwishin and their visitors—our DCC groups—were discovering how organizations such as Ayumpum and the World Dream Institute can build bridges of mutual respect and shared learning between cultures that are far apart both geographically and philosophically. On our next trip to the Amazon, we would learn how they could also unite two neighboring tribes that had been deadly enemies for centuries.

The Shaman's Journey
in the Words of **Daniel Wachapa**

Although my parents were poor by modern standards—like those
I've seen when I've traveled to the United States with Dream
Change Coalition—they honored our culture, customs, and language.
I believe they were wealthy in these ways, living the traditional
Shuar life. Like many men of his generation, my father was married
to two women. He was a powerful shaman. He and my mother were
both killed by another shaman out of jealousy, so as a very young
child I became an orphan.

Even though I know that my parents would have raised me well, I
cannot thank them for the kind of life I had. They were simply not
there for me. I had to make an effort to educate myself and decided
I needed to become a modern Shuar. I entered the mission school,
but after I completed the sixth grade, there was no one to give me
further education, so I returned to my Shuar roots. I became a
hunter and cultivated a small farm.

When I was sixteen, those who had killed my parents came after
me. That's the price of being the son of a great shaman! Looking for
a way to save my life, I fled from the lands of my family, leaving our
home behind. I wandered from community to community and spent a
lot of time in the forest. I know now that it was all part of my
education. I learned a great deal about life and facing up to enemies.

Two years later, when I was about eighteen, I became determined
to seek the power of arutam. I took great care in preparing
ayahuasca and tobacco. I followed a river until I arrived at a beach
where I stopped for the night. I was alone. It was there that I
decided to initiate myself; I took the ayahuasca.

After, I wandered along the shore of the river. Suddenly a great
vulture—a condor—appeared on the beach in front of me. We call
this bird Ayumpum, the same as the god who taught the Shuar about
ayahuasca and brought us enlightenment. I knew what I had to do. I

threw a stone to it and watched it take flight. As it soared over me, it vomited a piece of meat. I considered this a talisman, and, seizing the meat, I swallowed it.

Returning to the place I had selected on the beach, I sniffed my tobacco and lay down to journey. The vulture returned. She was huge, a true Ayumpum! She called out to me and said: "You will be an arutam man, but your path will not be that of the warrior. You have a mission you will know later. Fast, if you want luck and to be as strong as I am." I did all that the vulture told me to do. With Ayumpum's help, I became initiated.

Yet, it was only the beginning of an adventure that still continues. When I was about twenty years old, I had another important dream. I saw a man who looked something like an Evia. He was white like an Evia and much taller than I, but not as tall as an Evia. In my dream, he told me that my mission in life was to teach him and his people and also to help the forests and the animals. It was a powerful dream that I never forgot, although at the time it made no sense to me.

When I was thirty years old and married, I wanted to set my wife up and create a future for my children. I returned home. For four years we lived well, and my children attended the mission school. Then the old troubles came back to haunt me—the shaman's jealousy all over again. Two of my children grew terribly sick. We called on the help of friendly shamans; they and the herbal healers did their best, but we all knew the problems were caused by the jealous shaman's hatred.

Once again I decided to leave. I looked for a piece of virgin land where I could start a community. I built a longhouse; my wife and I established beautiful gardens, including a banana orchard. Eventually, two other families joined us. We decided to create a community where we could have a school for our children. Then suddenly, mysteriously, I became sick.

On the verge of dying, I was taken out of the jungle by a missionary, to the hospital in Shell. What a shock! I saw people who looked like the man I had dreamed of all those years ago—white people who looked like smaller versions of the Evias. They were doctors and missionaries from the United States. They did many things, gave me foul-tasting medicines, but nothing stopped my illness. I decided to leave the hospital and return to the forest.

There I turned to a shaman, who began his work on me. We took a great deal of ayahuasca and flew together. Such amazing journeys! In the process, we shared many of my past experiences; he saw clearly the history of my life. After several weeks with him, I was completely recovered.

The shaman asked something of me in return for the healing he had performed. He told me I must train with him, that my dreams about the vulture and my sickness were omens telling me that I needed to become a shaman, to heal people and teach others about the traditional ways of the Shuar.

As you know, learning to be a shaman is very difficult and painful. When my teacher planted the invisible darts, tsentsak, in my heart, I grew terribly ill; however, at least this time I understood the reason: the darts were becoming one with me and were multiplying inside my heart. I trained and trained, and eventually I became a very powerful shaman.

At the age of forty, I traveled to Miazal, near where the shaman Chumpi lived. There I met John Perkins. I recognized him immediately—he was the man in my dream! At that time, Chumpi was preparing to shapeshift out of human form. I understood then that my mission was to help this gringo and to teach his people, exactly as I'd been told in my dream twenty years earlier. I've seen how much help those people from North America need, how little they know about the world, how sincere they are in wanting to understand.

After several years of working with the Dream Change groups, I went to a conference in the United States arranged by John and Dr. Eve Bruce. It took me two weeks to get from my home to the airport in Los Angeles. There I was amazed by the type of lives people lead, the immensity of their homes, the cars and roads, and how far removed they are from the animals and plants. John and Eve and I traveled all around the country.

One time we stayed for several days in a house near Chicago, a house as big as fifteen or twenty Shuar longhouses—with a swimming pond inside it and great glass walls that looked up into the sky. I'd never dreamed a house could be so huge! The woman who lived there spoke some Spanish and liked to talk with me. She was very nice and an excellent cook. She told me that little animals, sort of like guinea pigs, were destroying her garden and asked what I would do if it happened at my home. I pointed at the large dog who slept inside her house near the kitchen stove, and I mentioned the two cats. I couldn't believe they would allow these little animals in the garden.

"On, no," she said. "They don't hunt!"

Her words amazed me. I couldn't understand—dogs and cats who don't hunt, who don't protect the home and gardens! Later on, John showed me some cookies that were shaped like bones and told me they were for the dog. No wonder he doesn't hunt! How very strange.

I've gained all the powers promised to me in the vision of ayahuasca during my initiation journey with the condor all those years ago. Now I continue working with the spirits of the forests and fulfilling my mission with the people from the North.

I only want to add this: The most important thing in life is to have faith, to believe in the spiritual ancestors, arutam, what the missionaries call the Almighty God. Our ancestors had faith in the goddess Nunqui, who was Mother Earth. Because they had faith and respected Mother Earth, they lived well and they ate what Mother Earth provided. I know from working with the people John brings that many have difficulty with this. They talk about faith, yet teach their children that they must learn to conquer the world around them rather than trust in the Almighty. They teach about planning but only planning for the short term. They don't teach the importance of looking out for the time of our grandchildren—a very greedy attitude that says, "Don't have faith, don't consider the harm your actions may cause in the long term, only plan for your own selfish benefit." But that's a foolish lesson, destined to bring great sorrow.

Why do I stress the need for faith? Faith gives us arutam. When we have faith, we know no fear. It's one of the reasons we shamans use ayahuasca. This most sacred of the plants lifts the top off our heads, allowing the fear to escape and the faith to pour in. Then we're invincible. It's why the Shuar have never been conquered by anyone. Not even today.

Sowing the Spirit
of the Shuar

"**M**onster anacondas live in that river." The Achuar warrior pointed with his single-shot, muzzle-loaded musket at the broad waters of the Pastaza River. "Man-eaters! I wouldn't swim there if I were you."

We huddled closer together, glancing around at each other, eleven adults and my thirteen-year-old daughter, Jessica. Fear, mixed with the exhaustion of a long, stressful trip into the Forbidden Territory, seemed as palpable as the humid jungle air.

We had traveled far that day: a bone-jarring, predawn bus ride down a tortuous Andean road; a mad dash through torrential rains at the airstrip; a wait that seemed like days while the skies cleared enough to fly; a gut-wrenching flight on three small planes; a trek along a jungle trail into an Achuar community that had never seen a group of outsiders before; and a drenching canoe journey. At last, late in the afternoon, we had arrived at our destination, a small clearing in the steamy jungle swamplands.

Unlike the mountainous Miazal area, this was a place where the intense tropical heat was unrelenting—an area infested with malarial mosquitoes and river life that made swimming treacherous: anacondas; stingrays; piranhas; and tiny umbrella fish that had a nasty habit of swimming up human urinary tracts, spreading their parasol-like gills, and lodging themselves so securely that only surgery could relieve their unfortunate victims. However, we had been told—and I could confirm from the last trip's experiences—that at this particular spot in the river we were safe from stingrays, piranhas, and, if we swam in bathing trunks or underwear, the umbrella fish. The only thing we needed to fear were the anacondas!

I looked closely at the others. I had to wonder whether I was just imagining their fear, projecting my own anxieties onto them. It struck me as almost comical that I, who had been visiting such places for three decades, should be so nervous; but every time I looked at Jessica, I saw Winifred reminding me that I was taking our daughter, our only child, into a dangerous place.

I knew that no member of our group was faint of heart. Each had felt the thrill of adventure before this. Each had been advised of the risks long before signing up. Bill and Lynne Twist; Bob and Wendy Graham; Dave Ellis and his wife, Trisha Waldron; Josh Mailman; Jim Gollin; Deb Imershein; Ella Alford; and Jessica, who had visited Latin American outposts many times during her young life: all had come in spite of the dangers—or, perhaps, because of them—and now we were here, on a mission of mercy, responding to a request the Achuar had made.

Achuar Tribal Council

It had happened at a council meeting held when Ehud, Juan Gabriel, and I had visited Danny Koupermann and the Achuar after we left Tukupi. The elders told us they had heard about the projects Dream Change Coalition had undertaken with the Shuar. They knew that Mary Tendall was working with a young uwishin, Yajanua Maria Arcos, and that together they had created the Seed Project, which was helping Shuar women distribute and sell to upscale U.S. shops the sustainable jewelry they crafted; that Mary and Peem were planning to produce a CD and video that would make traditional Shuar music available to the world; and that DCC trips were bringing people and cash into Miazal in an environmentally nondestructive way. They told us they had also heard that Shuar shamans had begun to travel abroad, sharing their wisdom with people in other countries, and about a DCC project that was helping to protect the sacred forests, plants, and animals in other parts of Ecuador (although at that time POLE had not yet reached Miazal, it was conserving Andean cloud forests).

One by one, the Achuar elders had stood, glanced around at their peers, and addressed us, their visitors. Each expressed concern about the tribe's prospects as it entered the modern world of airstrips, mission schools, and economic development. Together they pleaded with us to help them in ways similar to those we had introduced to the Shuar.

"We are poor," one of the elders said. A gnarled cane supported him as he rose to his feet. "We don't have airplanes, but we know things. We're not stupid. We've survived long in these forests and have learned much. We can offer you what we know, in return for your help."

"But we do need your advice," another echoed. "How can we deal with the oil men, the cattle and lumber companies? We have no experience there.

"Now that the missionaries, teachers, and doctors come, more of our babies live; we all have longer lives. But we're threatened with starvation. We can't always feed our families by hunting—too many people, too little game. We must get down on our knees and beg for handouts. This is not the Achuar way. The white man is making us his slave. While he didn't defeat us with weapons, he's done so with books and medicines. We need people like you who can think like the whites and also be one with us.

"We here are a small circle." The elder opened his hands and moved them slowly around the room, encompassing Achuar and outsider alike. "You started with a small circle of Shuar, too—and look what's happened! It's appropriate that we benefit from what the Shuar learned. Although we've been longtime enemies, we must all band together now to protect these lands. Please, we ask you, form a new circle in your North America community and let them unite with this circle here. Come to our aid, and we'll give back something powerful in return.*

Once again, the circle seemed to be the key. Ehud and I discussed the possibilities over the next few days. Danny and Juan Gabriel urged us to do whatever we could. For his part, Danny expressed his willingness to devote himself to the Achuar cause and to bring in a friend, Arnaldo Rodriquez, an Ecuadorian biologist and rain forest specialist. I knew that the DCC people who were working with the Shuar were already overextended. The Achuar

---

*For more details on meetings with the Achuar, see *Shapeshifting*, Destiny Books, Rochester, VT: 1997, chapter 15.

had requested a new circle, and it was apparent that it was needed on our end, too—fresh colleagues who could benefit from our experiences with the Shuar but would not be constrained by them.

Ehud encouraged me to look to Social Ventures Network. Founded by Josh Mailman, SVN provides a forum for bringing individuals with socially and environmentally responsible ideas together with those who have money to invest in such ideas. Ehud was a founding member and saw to it that I was quickly inducted. It was through SVN that I met Lynne and Bill Twist.

The Twists had an impressive record of raising money for good causes. After getting to know them, I became convinced that they might hold the key to helping the Achuar. Although neither had ever been to South America before, they were intrigued with the idea of taking an expedition deep into the Amazon, to places white men had never explored. Together we assembled a small group of SVN members to make the journey.

Anaconda and Evias

Now, here we were—a group of exhausted, sweaty, well-intentioned gringos standing on the bank of the great Pastaza River, headwater of the Amazon, glancing around furtively at one another, each of us facing our own fears, sweltering in the heat, wondering whether or not to tempt the anacondas.

"I'm hot enough to brave almost anything," Bill said.

"Come on, Daddy." Jessica pulled my arm. "It looks okay." She released me and wandered closer to the river.

Conversation ceased. We stood there together, watching Jessica and silently observing the river, mesmerized by the muddy current as it swept Andean soils, jungle muck, and debris on an odyssey to the Atlantic Ocean some three thousand miles away. I could not help marveling at how different this river was from those in the Cutucú. Gone were the waterfalls, the steep, rocky banks, the dense jungle cut here and there by Shuar trails, and the crystal-clear water. These had been replaced by vast floodplains inhabited by gigantic palms—pathless lands, impenetrable by foot, where even the most skilled hunters traveled by canoe, and water that was closer to the color of bloodstained earth than that of the sky.

Suddenly our reverie was interrupted by a shriek. I was stunned to discover that it came from Jessica. She was struggling with something by the river, fighting to keep from being dragged into the water!

I raced toward her. Then I stopped. I saw Josh. On his belly, writhing like a snake, he was clutching her by the ankle. For the briefest instant I wished a genuine anaconda would rise up and grab him! I looked around. Everyone was laughing. The episode had served to transform our anxieties into mirth. Maybe we really did need a swim to wash away the heat and grime and to shapeshift our fears.

I approached the Achuar warrior. He was an uwishin in his own right, a man perhaps in his mid-fifties who had worked many years for the missionaries and had been given the name Walter. He was considered to be one of the greatest hunters in the territory, and I asked him how grave the danger really was.

"Anacondas sometimes eat people," he said matter-of-factly. "It's happened in this river—to adults as well as children."

This was not what I was hoping to hear. "Walter, you know how long we've been traveling. The lake where we swam last time I was here is too low now. We're terribly hot and sweaty."

He looked me over carefully. "If you didn't wear so many clothes, you'd be better off." Then he glanced at his own outfit. "Me, too. Now that I work as a guide, I wear boots and shorts—and even this silly T-shirt." Emblazoned across it were the words *101 Dalmatians*. "Why do the missionaries insist on these foolish things?" I had no answer for that one. He laughed. Then his expression turned serious. "If you just want to bathe, maybe it can work." He took a deep breath and looked around. "See that canoe down there, tied to the tree, one end on the beach and the other sticking out into the river? It gets deep very fast. The far end of the canoe is way over your head. Even for the tall guy." He indicated Bill. "Keep your hands on the canoe and be ready to jump into it. I'll go up there." With his musket he pointed at a small hill, an outcropping that hung above the river. "I'll probably see any anaconda swimming down river before it reaches you." His wrinkled features broke into a grin. "Just don't tempt it—when I holler, you leap into the canoe."

I took the good news back to the group. Several shook their heads or muttered under their breaths and wandered off. Lynne, Jessica, Bill, Josh, Jim, and I stripped down to our underwear or bathing suits and stepped into the water.

I was shocked by the ferocity of the current. We were at the outside of a big bend in the river, where the water flowed very swiftly. After taking several steps, my feet were swept out from beneath me. I grabbed the canoe with one hand and Jessica around the waist with the other.

"Let's go back, Daddy," she pleaded. "I think I'm clean enough now."

Just then something struck my leg, something hard, rough-skinned, and rounded—like the side of a giant snake! All around me the others were screaming. I rushed to push Jessica into the canoe. Whatever it was in the water rose up and brushed across my thigh. Jessica slipped out of my grasp and back into the river. Next to her, the water rippled violently, and something dark and hairy broke the surface. I struggled desperately to get her into the canoe, but I was too late—the thing that had been submerged now exploded from the current: Jim's head. He panted for air. "A log," he gasped. "It was just an old log that got stuck under the canoe."

Once again we all began to laugh, but it was cut short by Walter's shouting. He motioned for us to climb into the canoe, and we obeyed immediately. He came down to the edge of the bank and wanted to know what all the commotion had been about. When I explained, he did not seem amused.

"Enough bathing." It was a statement. "Stay in the canoe," he ordered, "or come onto land." He turned abruptly and headed back to his lookout point.

We sat in the canoe, all six of us, and watched the current flow past. The water was littered with branches—twigs as small as toothpicks, trunks as big around as the canoe and much longer—flowers, mosses, and all manner of rain forest matter. It seemed odd—the way we had been duped twice, panicked first by Josh, then a log. It seemed to echo something that had happened earlier in the day.

We had emerged from a jungle trail into an Achuar community never before visited by white people. Jessica had entered the clearing and headed straight for a cluster of children. When they spotted her, they stood there dumbstruck for a second—then, screaming "Evia, Evia!" took off into the forest and disappeared. She had returned to our group, looking forlorn and confused.

I hugged her and reminded her about the story of the Evias, explaining that perhaps these people had not yet heard the part about Etsaa destroying them. I pointed out that she was taller than most of their parents and that we adults must truly look like giants. Everyone around us laughed, and soon Jessica joined in.

Then Lynne turned her gently back toward the clearing, facing the sun. She pointed at Jessica's mouth. "Your braces!" she exclaimed. "Look at how they shine." We all peered at Jessica; in the bright light of the clearing her mouth appeared to be filled with gleaming knives more threatening than the jaws of any piranha. "No wonder those kids thought you were a terrible monster!"

Sitting in the canoe, I reminded the others of this incident. "Amazing," I said, "the way our own actions in the water a few minutes ago mirror the kids' reaction to Jessica's braces. We thought they were so funny, running away from Jessica, that the Achuar seem very provincial—but so far we've been absolutely convinced that both Josh and a log were anacondas!"

"I guess it's all a matter of perspective," someone added.

"Come on!" Walter shouted. "Rain." he pointed to the sky. An osprey circled directly above us; ominous dark clouds were massing along the horizon. "We should reach the shaman's house before it pours."

That night we participated in an ayahuasca ceremony with an Achuar shaman named Taish. He lived in a large, traditional longhouse with two wives and their families. Although Juan Gabriel, Danny, and I had shared the sacred teacher plant with him on our previous visit with Ehud, this time we refrained, as was our custom when we were leading groups. Not all of the others accepted Taish's offer, but for those who did, it was an extremely powerful night. They learned that their futures were, in fact, tied to the Achuar.

Ransom

I awoke the next morning wrapped in a sleeping bag next to Jessica's, the two of us beneath a mosquito net inside a small longhouse that had been loaned to our group by the Achuar. The netting felt odd to me, constraining, even offensive; but here along the Pastaza it protected us from mosquitoes and malaria. As my eyes adjusted to the light, I spied a brigade of them buzzing around the edges of the net.

Then I remembered that this was our last morning in the rain forest. We had chartered planes to fly in to a nearby landing strip and return us to the Andes—weather permitting. I listened for the sound of rain. Hearing none, I stretched and started to crawl out of the sleeping bag.

"Daddy—is that you?" Jessica rolled over and looked at me sleepily.

"No. The anaconda."

She punched me in the shoulder. "Is it breakfast time?"

"I'll check the weather." I unzipped the small opening and crept past the other netting tents scattered about the floor. Diffused light slanted in through the slits between the vertical bamboo slats that formed the walls of the longhouse. Even before I reached the door I knew I'd find sunshine. I stepped outside. The sun was perched atop the trees in front of me, the sky overhead cloudless. I felt an immediate sense of relief—it was a good day for flying.

A flock of macaws soared past; their brilliant reds flashed like flames against the azure sky. Then my heart sank as they faded into the thunderheads piling up along the western horizon. I rushed back inside and clapped my hands.

"Time to get up," I shouted. "The weather's perfect for flying right now, but it won't be for long." We had explained earlier that the pilots could not afford to allow their planes to get socked in by bad weather; if rain threatened and they did not see us waiting for them when they flew over the landing strip, they would leave for another assignment—and might not return for days.

The group was quick to respond. Even those who had taken ayahuasca rose and dressed immediately. Within minutes all of them were rolling up their sleeping bags and mosquito nets. Danny built a fire in the lean-to next door that had been designated as our kitchen. Lucho, an Ecuadorian cook who had accompanied many DCC groups, hurriedly prepared pancake batter.

I had promised Jessica that she and I would serve this last rain forest breakfast, paying special attention to those who were recovering from the ceremony of the night before. We bustled about, cutting leaves to use as plates and conjuring knives and forks from the depths of backpacks.

Suddenly there was a loud shout from outside our longhouse. Lucho answered it. A young Achuar warrior rushed inside, seeming very perturbed.

After handing a note to Danny, he immediately dashed out. There were no salutations, no greetings, no handshakes or questions about how we felt. Danny, Juan Gabriel, Lucho, and I exchanged glances. This unusual conduct was not a good sign

We all crowded around Danny. He unfolded the note and read it to himself—and then his face turned white. He passed the note to Juan Gabriel.

Juan Gabriel took a long time with it. Finally he looked at me, avoiding the gaze of all the others. He spoke in Spanish so they would not understand him. "I don't know what do. It's terrible," he said.

"Why don't you read it aloud," I suggested. "In English."

"I can't." He handed it to me.

Aware that the tension was now approaching panic, I immediately read it to the group, translating the words from Spanish to English as I went along. "People who took ayahuasca last night owe the shaman $1000 (U.S.!). Pay before you leave this community."

There were gasps. I was speechless.

"Ransom," someone said.

Another added, "We're hostages!"

Seeds Planted

On our earlier trip, when Ehud, Juan Gabriel, and I had taken ayahuasca with Taish, he had charged us nothing. However, we had left food, mosquito netting, flashlights, and batteries with him as an exchange. This new demand seemed outrageous!

Aware that the window of opportunity for arriving at the landing strip in time to catch our planes was rapidly closing, we sent word to the shaman and the rest of the community that we needed to hold a meeting—right away. We knew from past experience that we were unlikely to reach a quick resolution unless the whole community was involved and everyone was given the chance to express an opinion.

In the midst of all the confusion, Jessica took my hand and pulled me aside. "You promised to serve breakfast with me, Daddy."

"But, Jessica, this is an emergency. I have to go to the meeting." I looked at the disappointment in her face—the face of both a child and a young woman—seeing then that this joint breakfast effort was even more important to her than I realized. "I'll make it up to you. I promise." I'm not sure, though, that she ever really forgave me. She had worked very hard during the trip to help me, and this had been the only request she made in return. It was an incident I would remember vividly five years later, on the day Winifred and I left her waving to us from the doorway of her dorm, a freshman about to start college, farther from home, it seemed to me, than even the Amazon.

When we arrived at the longhouse where the meeting was to be held, we were greeted in the normal cordial fashion. Chicha was passed. Taish inquired about the people who had taken ayahuasca and appeared pleased to learn that they had all had powerful experiences. It seemed a painfully slow process, but, like Danny and Juan Gabriel, I knew we had no choice. In the end, our patience paid off.

As it turned out, Taish had no idea what one thousand U.S. dollars were worth; it had simply been a number one of his sons who attended a mission school had come up with, loosely based on one thousand *sucres,* the currency of Ecuador, which, at the time, was valued at seven thousand sucres to the dollar! We agreed on a fair price and used it to establish a standard for future trips. The incident became a sort of joke, a subject for cocktail parties—however, it was an important lesson; it served notice about the magnitude of the problems confronting the Achuar as they struggled to enter the modern world.

It also created an unexpected side benefit. The next morning, the group's last in Ecuador, we were back in the Andes. During breakfast at our hotel, Dave Ellis, the author of highly regarded books about empowerment, suggested we assemble for a brief discussion.

Dave opened by pointing out that many of us had recently been granted a reprieve from paying one thousand dollars, and he thought it appropriate that we donate that money to finance a new organization for building bridges between the Achuar and North Americans. He went around the circle of SVN members, asking each how much additional money he or she would be willing to contribute. Within fifteen minutes we had raised $118,000 (U.S.!).

Bill Twist volunteered to take the next step, which began an incredible process. Within a couple of years the Twists and many other dedicated people built up an organization, which they named The Pachamama Alliance (TPA). Based on principles and a mission statement that reflect those of DCC—including a commitment to follow the POLE example of using forests to offset greenhouse gases—TPA has forged a partnership with the Achuar. It is helping them to fulfill the dreams they expressed during those meetings attended by Ehud, Juan Gabriel, Danny, and me after we had visited their enemy, Tukupi.

For DCC the process is a wonderful confirmation of the power of working in nonhierarchical structures. We sat in a circle—many circles, held discussions with people from diverse cultures, and made decisions. We planted a seed and allowed it room to grow. The right people stepped forward and took responsibility for protecting and nurturing the seedling, helping it to reach up and stretch its branches out to Etsaa, the sun. The history of The Pachamama Alliance is an example of how indigenous concepts can be applied to solve problems confronting the modern world. It is illustrative of the power inherent in an organization that, like DCC, is modeled on ancient tribal principles.

Another seed had sprouted from that earlier trip to the Forbidden Territory. Ehud was impressed with the Italian missionary who came to our rescue at Tukupi's house, not solely because he managed to start our plane's engine. The ever-vigilant publisher had been struck by what the missionary told us about collecting Shuar stories for his order. He said, "I am committed to not just converting them to Catholicism; I want to make sure that Catholics learn from them as well."

That chance encounter inspired Ehud with the idea that resulted in this book. He called me one day to discuss it, and when I heard the excitement in his voice, I knew this was not simply a cordial call. "Why don't you enlist your amikri to interview the people of Miazal? Give him a small tape recorder. Send him out to the shamans, the old people who won't be around much longer. They embody the spirit of the Shuar. Convince him to get them to talk about it." He paused. "Remember what Peem said. You should only agree to accept the amikri honor if you will need his help and have something to offer him in return."

"He helps me every time I take trips there—and I bring him things and plan on having my godson live with us someday."

"Of course. But there's more. What does he need right now?"

This was before the formation of the Ayumpum Foundation and the introduction of POLE to the Miazal area. There could be only one answer to Ehud's question. "He needs cash," I admitted, thinking of our last conversation when Mariano confessed to me that he was considering turning a small portion of his forests into pastures so that he could raise a couple of calves, sell them as cows, and accumulate the money necessary to buy the clothes and shoes Pascualina required in order to attend the mission school. He also needed to repair his broken musket.

"Exactly. And it really fits in with the whole amikri idea, the modern notion of trading ideas, not just salt and blowguns. Pay him for his efforts, pay the uwishin he interviews. But remember that all of you are doing the Shuar a big favor by helping them honor and retain stories and traditions that are extremely important to them."

"And us."

"That's my point. Just like the Italians, the Catholics, we all need to hear the wisdom of their culture. That missionary told us the Shuar are the last unconquered people of the Amazon, at least the last tribe of magnitude, one that can claim to be like a nation. How have they done it? What's their secret? Let's have them tell us about it—and everybody wins."

Secrets

On my next trip to Miazal, I discussed the idea with Mariano and a number of the uwishin. They embraced it wholeheartedly. Some of the North Americans who had come with me had their doubts, though. "What about the secrets?" one asked.

"What secrets?" Daniel Wachapa replied.

"Your shamanic secrets."

"We don't have any."

"But," another member of our group protested, "North American indigenous people are very protective of their ceremonies and techniques."

"Why?" Tuntuam asked.

"They say we steal their knowledge from them."

The shamans all looked at each other dubiously.

"How can you steal what belongs to all of us?" Daniel finally asked.

"They are your traditions, not ours."

"We are all here together, all brothers and sisters." He smiled. "The only way these rain forests will survive is if you people change your dreams. For too long you've been separated from your hearts and the spirits, you've lost the trail to arutam. Therefore, we must help you, guide you back onto that trail. How can we do this if we think about secrets?"

"There are no secrets," Tuntuam reaffirmed. "Everything we know comes from Nunqui, Tsunkqui, Etsaa, the anaconda and jaguar. It's spoken by Nase, the healing wind in the forests."

They all glanced at me and laughed—Nase is the name they had given me.

"When Nase speaks, we all listen!" Peem stood up and slapped me on the back.

"Truly," Daniel said, "the message carried on the wind is meant to be heard by everyone."

"Why isn't everyone a shaman, then?" one of our group asked.

"Everyone has that power," Daniel answered. "But it's a difficult life, full of hard work and danger. Not many want to take it on."

Back in the United States, Wendy Graham, one of the participants on the trip to the Achuar, offered to pay for tape recorders, cassettes, and batteries. My father, an eighty-three-year-old retired Spanish teacher, volunteered to translate the tapes from Spanish to English. His granddaughter, Jessica, agreed to type his handwritten pages into the computer.

And so the seed for this book was sown.

▲ ▲

Progress and Development

in the Words of
Yajanua Maria Arcos, Yaanua Patricia, and Mariano

Yajanua Maria Arcos: My father, Juan Arcos, founded this community. He came here some twenty-five years ago to establish a church and school. My mother, Amalia Tuitza, is a great herbal healer. My sister, Yaanua, and I studied with her often during our lives and continue to learn from her. Maria is my Spanish name; my Shuar name, Yajanua, means Far-away Woman. Yaanua means Star Woman. I went to college in Quito, so I've seen both sides of the river—ours, the Shuar side, and yours, the "developed" side.

Yaanua Patricia: Now that I've lived for thirty-three years, I can look back and say that our childhood was beautiful beyond belief. We had the opportunity to share the wonders and spirit of the forest, learning to live as one with all the animals and plants—each species taught us something different. These are very special relationships that endure all our lives. Now I try to pass this wisdom on to my three children.

Yajanua: We Shuar know that we are inseparable from nature, strands in the same spider's web. We believe that all the men who were powerful when they were alive on earth are transformed into powerful animals when they die. They live in the jungle as spirits, and they live in the waterfall. That's why the Shuar go to the waterfall—to be able to see these great men, to acquire their strength and energy.

Yaanua: We believe in the power of the ancestors, the spirit world and arutam. They're everything to us, comforting and protecting us. These ideas bring us joy.

I've also had the opportunity to know the world outside the jungle. I went to college in Quito like my sister and then traveled to Europe, where I married an Austrian man. Now I work closely with the groups Dream Change brings in here. Wow, how different people can be! The North Americans and Europeans have a completely different view of the world!

Yajanua: You people in the North call yourselves "developed." You say you come from the "developed" countries, so I'll use these words as well. You believe that your civilization has developed for many thousands of years, that you can look back to ancient cultures in Asia and the Middle East and trace this development through Europe and into the United States. You say you've made great progress—and this is true in many ways. You also look at us, at the Shuar and other indigenous people, and you say that we haven't developed, that we've been static, that our lives are "primitive." The idea of being primitive has begun to appeal to some of your people in recent years, some of the ones who come here—but it simply isn't true that we're primitive. Look around you. We don't live like the Shuar of a thousand years ago—or the Shuar of my parents' generation. And I'm not referring to the things you brought us, the clothes, radios, and airplanes. We've always developed. Talk to our wisest elders, the uwishin. They'll tell you the truth about this.

Every generation of Shuar since the time of Tuntiak in the beginning has progressed. We've cultivated forest plants, learned new ways to fish and hunt, adapted to floods and droughts; our shamans are constantly understanding new things about healing, journeying, and employing the power of our herbs. This was going on long before the white man ever came here, long before the Spanish Conquest of the Andes. It's not as you think, that you've progressed and we haven't. We've developed, too—but the difference is in the way it has happened.

Our way has always taken into account all other life forms and the lives of our children's children. This includes the spirits and the ancient ones, our ancestral spirits. All of that's part of who we are today. For us the word "progress" does not apply if it threatens other species or could possibly harm future generations—or if it ignores the spirits. How could that be progress?"

We've developed in parallel to you—only we've done it very, very differently. But now, all that's changing. The "developed" world has introduced materialistic ideas. The young Shuar are tempted by brightly colored T-shirts and wristwatches. They want to learn to fly airplanes and drive cars.

Yaanua: If I compare life today with what it was here in the jungle thirty years ago, I see many changes. I always find myself asking, "Why? Why does it have to change so much?" I remember how wonderful it used to be.

In my childhood we were free. There were no worries about being imprisoned in a schoolroom, cut off from the jungle. Instead we went fishing with our mothers. Of course, that changed even when I was little. I ended up going to school, too. But even that was different from the way it is for my children now. School was smaller, more basic. We spent a lot of time in the forest.

Yajanua: Our father was responsible for this mission; he was its founder. He made sure we went to school. But our mother was 100 percent Shuar. She made sure that we learned to be good Shuar women.

Yaanua: Shuar women manage the households. We bring balance. But Papa realized that for Shuar women to retain our power, our arutam, our place of honor in the family, we would have to integrate into modern society. So he emphasized the importance of education for us.

He sent me away from here, to a school far away, when I was about thirteen. I lived with my older sister and her family. I was distressed by this. I used to wonder why I couldn't stay in the jungle. I worried that Papa didn't love me anymore, and I looked forward to the vacations, when I could return home.

With the passage of time, however, I realized that my parents did love me, that they sent me away to study because they wanted this Shuar woman to continue playing the role of a powerful woman in the future, to bring balance to the new world that was spreading into our homeland, deep into the jungle.

Yajanua: Our mother reflects the old ways, the type of progress I mentioned earlier. She's an amazing woman, a great herbal healer and shaman.

Yaanua: You can't lie to her because she can tell from your eyes whether you're telling the truth or are trying to deceive her. Even with strangers, she can tell.

She knows so many plants and how they're used. She learned from her mother and grandmother and then she expanded the knowledge. She teaches what she knows to us—I hope someday to know as much as she does so I can carry on this knowledge and pass it along to my children. She also uses her body as a learning tool. She has a small vein in her leg that throbs when she asks it questions. Depending on how the vein reacts, she can predict what will happen. She knows whether the plane will arrive on a certain day, even who will be on the plane. She's never wrong.

Mariano: I can tell you that doña Amalia, Yaanua's mother, didn't learn about the plants in school—or how to listen to the messages of her body. The Shuar children of the past, like her generation, didn't go to schools. But they knew a great deal, things that are forgotten today.

When Spanish-speaking people arrived here, they brought priests and established missions and schools. At first we Shuar didn't trust the missionaries, but they gave us machetes and pots—things that changed our lives. They also told us the stories of Christ and the miracles of the Bible. These aren't unlike our own legends. After a while, we grew accustomed to the missionaries and began to see that it might be useful to educate our children—at least for them to learn Spanish.

Schools open a door for our children, so that they'll have choices later in life. They can become whatever they want, like children in other countries: pilots, mechanics, businessmen, bus drivers, even doctors and lawyers. They can make money and live in far-off places, if they decide to. Those possibilities depend on education. Without it, who are we as far as the rest of the world is concerned?

Today, money has become important, even necessary. We can't send our children to school without clothes and books—it's not allowed. And these things cost money. The forests are being destroyed around us, the game and fish are sometimes scarce, even the fruits. Without an education, how will our children eat?

Our diet is changing with education. We're beginning to eat animals that aren't native to the jungle, like the chickens we raise. The money coming in with the foreigners is altering our lives. Now we're dependent on things from the outside to maintain our families—you know, knives, shot for our guns, flashlights, batteries, clothes, and boots. Money buys them. Even health and medicines can be bought with money. We need money to purchase calves. Then we have to cut our precious trees to create pastures so that we can sell the full-grown cows for a profit. We hate to cut the trees, but what choice do we have? Raising cattle has become our only form of banking. More and more every year, money increases in importance. Without money, no calves that grow to cattle; without cattle, we can't provide for our families.

Really, this is the plight of the Shuar culture. Many of us are very poor. When one of us doesn't have cattle, pigs, or chickens, no one is going to give us the things we need. Without money, we're nothing in this new, modern world. With it, we have a chance.

We're just now beginning this new program called POLE. My amikri brought it to us. It offers hope that we can preserve our forests and still earn enough cash to provide for our families.

Yaanua: The forests are disappearing. People—not just colonists, but other Shuar—are moving in. They come from the Upano Valley and places where the jungle has already been destroyed. They move here in order to escape the urbanization. But this means that now we're getting more and more settlers in this area. Oh, there's still plenty of jungle! But how long will it last? Yes, people need cash today—even the most remote Shuar. They cut the trees in order to raise cattle, to earn money. But where will it stop? My generation, the new generation of leaders, must change.

I want my children to have the same opportunities that I've had, to live free, and to be free to love and prosper in this beautiful forest. In spite of the many marvels I've seen in other parts of the world, this is the best! It's a simple life, and the best. How can man create a garden to compare with this one that Nunqui created for us? That's why I've brought my children back here, to learn and live as I did—to be free.

Yajanua: What's going to happen to the Shuar people in the future? It's very difficult to say. Unfortunately we're seeing so much change, materialism that the outside world has brought to us.

Yaanua: If we don't take care of the very thing that gives us life, feeds and shelters us, and provides our water and air, we shall die with it, all of us. When the spirit of the forest ceases, the spirit of the Shuar will be gone forever. And so too the spirit of all people. We must protect our forests. If we cut trees, we must replant.

Yajanua: Nowadays everyone is a materialist. That's what bothers me the most. We all do everything for money. Why do we feel this way? Because we've lost touch with our ancestral spirits. If we don't change what's inside—the spirit—and if we don't try to help others change, at least a little bit, we'll all be finished. The environment is not separate from us; it is us.

Epilogue

Rain pelted the palms like a hail of bullets. The wind, Nase, whipped the river into frothy, liquid likenesses of snowcapped peaks while lightning sliced through thick blankets of dark clouds. It was a day that harked back to the time when Etsaa sent his brother, Ayumpum, down to earth on a lightning bolt to connect the people with Shakaim, the spirit of the forests, and enlighten them to the ecstasy of their oneness with nature.

A mangy dog crept along the outside wall, hugging it, protected from the rain by the overhanging eaves. I watched her as, tail between her legs, she warily eyed the puddle that threatened to enter the room where I sat listening to Peem strumming a soulful tune on his tumank.

The room was empty except for a television monitor, a table with a CD player, and a porcelain crucifix hanging on the wall. It was a large room—big enough to hold the seventy people who would attend DCC's annual Intensive Shapeshifting workshop—the meeting hall of a Catholic retreat center in Palm Beach Gardens, Florida. I was alone, save for the dog, the music, and the spirit of the crucifix.

The music of the tumank faded, and Peem's melodious voice rose above the sound of the rain, a hauntingly beautiful anent that brought tears to my eyes. Images from the past surfaced in my memory.

Mary Tendall stood before those participating in last year's workshop, describing her dream of taking a professional recording team into Miazal.

Amazingly, almost miraculously, the participants responded by raising the money needed to make it happen. The image shifted to Peem sitting before a fire, playing his tumank, composing a new anent whose notes could summon to reality the dream of oneness between cultures and between people and nature. His Shuar community responded happily by joining together to sing his anent as well as a collection of their traditional songs. Another shift to seventy-five children and adults walking into Miazal—some having trekked for hours through the jungle—to dust off their flutes, drums, and tumanks, instruments that had been played by grandparents and great-grandparents before them, and unite their hearts, souls, and voices to create this incredible CD of Shuar music.

Before me, on the floor, was an array of photographs Mary had taken during the Amazon recording sessions. I picked up one of them. The people of Miazal, the CD musicians and singers, had posed for a group shot. Dressed in the traditional clothes of the arutam Shuar, they seemed to be watching me as I sat in the Catholic retreat waiting to greet the other facilitators for this workshop. The women wore red and blue wraparound dresses tied over one shoulder. The men, topless, wore long ceremonial kilts and toucan-feather headdresses. All of them—men and women alike—had painted their faces and donned shacapa dance belts. Then I noticed something unusual. They were smiling! Although the Shuar are a very happy people who smile a lot, they seldom show this side of themselves to the camera. But they were doing it now, looking right at me and smiling. It was as though they too were waiting for the other workshop facilitators, members of our extended tribe—Bob, Cleicha, Eve, Ipupiara, Lyn, Mary, and Norma, and were smiling because they knew that we soon would be helping to pass along Shuar wisdom and spirit to the participants.

This photograph and the music playing in the background brought home to me the significance of the impact the Shuar are having. It had been ten years since Ehud and I first journeyed into Miazal and Juan Arcos requested: "Bring people here—not the ones who think they need to change us, but those who want to learn. Bring them here so they can feel the magic of our rivers and learn from uwishin about dreaming." Since that time over seven hundred people had gone with us to visit the Shuar. Every one of them felt that magic, I was certain. Many had returned home and taken it upon themselves to share the spirit of the Shuar with others, to change our collective dreaming.

During that first trip, Chumpi had summed up the Shuar philosophy: "We can always change the dream. It's easy." His words had seeded a movement that spread its branches to the world. DCC had given workshops and seminars to hundreds of thousands of people on five continents. But perhaps even more important was the fact that clans had sprung up everywhere— drumming circles of five or ten people, gatherings that attracted thousands of participants, and organizations that were creating an almost unimaginable variety of projects and programs. It was likely that some of these clan members had no idea that their roots reached back to the shores of the Mangosiza River; it was probable that they had never even heard of the Shuar or DCC. But it did not matter; what mattered was that the spirit was riding the wind—and taking root in many forms.

I recalled the words of the Dalai Lama as we flew together in a plane over the Himalayas, accompanied by twenty-nine other people on a DCC trip. "Keep following the example of your Shuar friends," he advised me. "Each of your members can directly influence ten, one hundred, or even one thousand others. Each of those people may then influence another ten, one hundred, or one thousand, and so forth." It reminded me of Peem's explanation of the amikri relationship. "Small circles expanding into larger ones," I said. The Dalai Lama nodded and smiled. "Exactly. A compassionate way to create change."

I set the group photograph back in its place and scanned the others. Another one caught my eye. Juan Arcos, the Catholic deacon who had brought the mission to Maizal three decades earlier, stood next to his wife, Amalia Tuitza, his daughter, Yaanua Patricia, and his son Peem. What was so amazing about this particular photograph was that don Juan Arcos was topless, wearing only a Shuar kilt, shacapa dance belt, toucan crown, and vermillion face paint. In his hand he held a chonta spear with a giant anaconda carved into its shaft. I knew that it was the first time he had dressed in the clothes of a traditional Shuar in over twenty-five years.

As I looked at this photograph I came to think of it as don Juan's conversion. Yet it was so much more. It symbolized a realization that he shared with a growing number of people that western development may not be the panacea we once thought it was. Don Juan, I felt, was demonstrating not just his approval for what his son had accomplished, but also admitting that the traditions of the Shuar are important to the world, acknowledging that the time has come when the uwishin must speak again—and the world needs to listen.

Rain hammered against the windows of the building. Outside, the palms were bowing like monks before an altar. Inside, Christ looked down at me from his porcelain cross.

Suddenly, I was transported back to the tiny Miazal church. Built Shuar-style, with walls of vertical palm staves pounded into the earth, it was decorated with blowguns, spears, turtle stools, and depictions of Nunqui who, carrying her baby, might have been mistaken for the Madonna.

"A nice place," Chumpi said. It had been our last afternoon together. "Quiet." He sat down on a turtle stool. "A good spot for shapeshifting, taking shamanic journeys."

I sat down beside him. Seeing all those Shuar artifacts in this place of Catholic worship, I was encouraged to ask a question that had been on my mind. "What if the Shuar had been the ones to travel the world, spreading the word?"

"Instead of the Catholics, you mean?"

I nodded.

His eyes held mine for a very long time. Then he glanced around the little room. "It's not our custom." His eyes returned to mine. "We defend ourselves against our enemies, but we don't try to convince them that our ways are superior. You can't force another person to arutam." He stood up and went to the church's central pole. A tapestry of the Shuar deities hung from it. He pointed at Etsaa blowing life back into the birds he had killed to feed the Evias. "Just as Etsaa had to meet the Evias alone, and just as he had to go down into the lake by himself to kill the monster anaconda, so must every one of us find our own arutam."

"But today these forests are threatened with destruction. The animals and plants, the Shuar—all of us—may face extinction."

"You're right," he agreed. "We must protect future generations of all our brothers and sisters. There is no peace without peace for all."

"Your teachings—Shuar teachings—might make that happen!"

He looked down at me from where he stood and chuckled. "If it's destined, then it will happen. Remember this, though—remember it always: It's spirit that empowers shapeshifts—ours and Shakaim's, the spirit of the forest." He raised his hand to his chest and spread the fingers wide. "Arutam is sown in the heart. The secret is not to preach to people but to help them open their hearts."

A Note from John Perkins on Storytelling and Translation

Shuar myths, legends, and history have endured throughout the ages because of a rich oral tradition. They have been passed down from one generation to the next during evenings of singing, dancing, talking, and drinking chicha around the fire. Only with the coming of the Europeans did the written language enter Shuar culture. Yet, even today, most of the uwishin do not read or write; nor do they speak any language other than Shuar.

The missionaries, who introduced an alphabet to the Shuar and taught the younger ones Spanish, in general were not interested in preserving the nuances of the Shuar language. Those few who tried soon discovered that the passions, poetry, and subtleties of indigenous storytelling are not easily converted to Spanish, Portuguese, English, or any of the European languages. To a certain extent, the spirit of the Shuar language is locked within the oral tradition.

When Mariano, Ehud, and I decided to compile this book we came face-to-face with the challenge of trying to bridge the language gap. We wanted to share the spirit of the Shuar—and their rich oral tradition—in writing and in languages that are not accustomed to describing such things as, for example, arutam. We recognized that the uwishin would assume that the listener understood many of the basic concepts of Shuar philosophy and religion—concepts that are quite foreign to the rest of the world. They would not pause in the middle of a story to explain the meaning of arutam or the importance of Nunqui. We also knew that they might be inhibited to a certain extent by the presence of a tape recorder and the inconvenience of having to pause frequently while Mariano translated into Spanish what they had just related in Shuar. So, how were we to help the reader understand the esoteric references and experience the passion of the story, while at the same time preserving the integrity of the speaker and his or her tale?

I took it upon myself to return to some of the epics I had read while an English major at Middlebury College (as it turned out, my editor at Inner Traditions, Elaine Sanborn, had also been an English major at Middlebury and shared my concerns and interest). I soon discovered that the translators of many of our oldest and most enduring works—*The Iliad, The Odyssey,* and *Beowulf,* to name a few—had been confronted by similar problems. Many had provided notes that were very helpful. In all the best cases— "best" by my personal evaluation as to the power and authenticity of the interpretations—the translators had not allowed themselves to be restricted by limitations of the written word. Rather, they had opted to try to elicit the true spirit of the work, to tell it as it might have been told by the bards and minstrels of the time—or, in my case, the uwishin sitting around a fire deep in the Amazon.

Taking these factors into account, we arrived at the following approach. Mariano would interview the uwishin in Shuar, except for those few younger ones who were fluent in Spanish. Using the tape recorder, he would immediately translate into Spanish. I would bring the tapes home to my father, Jason Perkins, a retired scholar, linguist, and Spanish teacher who, now in his mid-eighties, could be considered as a sort of uwishin to our culture. In longhand he painstakingly wrote out translations that were intended to be as literal as possible. This monumental task was complicated by the vast differences between Shuar and Spanish and because the Spanish itself was often flavored with words not found in any dictionary, ones that have evolved through the sometimes stormy relationship between Shuar people and Italian, Spanish, Belgian, and American missionaries. My daughter Jessica then transferred her grandfather's work to the computer. As a final step, I reviewed the tapes, turned to the computer, and tried to weave in the poetry and passions that have inspired me to listen to Shuar storytellers over the past three decades.

The fact that Shuar philosophy and mythology have been part of my life for years and that I have sat beside fires and heard most of the tales—in one form or another—many times before was an immeasurable help. There were times when I relied on these past experiences to fill in gaps or define concepts that might otherwise confuse the reader.

An interesting symmetry resulted from this process: Shuar elders, including Mariano's parents, gave their words to a young Shuar man; these same words were translated by a North American elder who passed them, through his granddaughter, to his own son. The nature of the material—especially those parts dealing with gender, sexual practices, initiations, and psychotropic plants—stimulated some fascinating discussions on the North American side and (I suspect) in the Amazon as well.

Originally the idea was simply to quote the Shuar, using a format similar to that of a theatrical script. However, Mariano asked that we include our side of the story also, the reasons for our interest in his culture, and the history of my personal involvement with his people. In addition, both Ehud and Elaine felt that the book needed a story line and atmosphere. Framing the Shuar discussions in the factual context of the trips and DCC history not only satisfied this need, it also provided a mechanism for explaining some of the esoteric references, defining words, and discussing the culture in terms intended to help outsiders gain a more complete appreciation for it.

Most of the Shuar dialogues were transcribed directly from the tapes. As with conversations among people on the DCC trips, a few were recreated from memory and notes jotted down in a journal or palm computer. In some instances, the cassette transcripts are intermingled with questions posed by facilitators or participants; rather than trying to reconstruct Shuar answers, I have relied on Mariano's taped interviews wherever possible. Thus, some of the text is a combination of recalled questions posed by visitors and answers that occurred during the recording sessions. In an attempt to keep the text flowing and organized by subject matter, meetings and conversations have sometimes been consolidated and are not always in the chronological order of their actual occurrence.

On a personal note I would like to add that during the past decade of facilitating shamanic and shapeshifting workshops, I have often found myself wondering whether I was exaggerating some of the things I said about the Shuar. I sometimes feared that I might be playing the old childhood game of "telephone" with myself, that something I said ten years ago had circulated around in my own subconscious and returned quite differently from how it had begun. Listening to the uwishin talk with my amikri and co-author, I have been gratified to learn that this was not the case. The truth of the Shuar—their spirit and the message they offer the rest of us—is far more fascinating than anything my imagination could possibly create.

 **Glossary**

amikri: The most important bond or relationship two Shuar men can share, one that is based on dedication and the vow of mutual help and support.

anents: Songs of the Shuar that, when sung, have the power to turn dreams into reality.

arutam: According to Shuar belief, the power or force that allows men to be successful warriors, husbands, and fathers, and women to excel in their duties as gardeners, mothers, and wives.

ayahuasca: *Natem,* in Shuar. The Quechua word for one of the sacred teacher plants, along with datura (maikiua) and tobacco, that is prepared and taken in order to reach a higher level of consciousness resulting in journeying, visions, transformation, and a deep sense of connection and oneness with the surrounding world.

Ayumpum: Etsaa's brother, the god of lightning, who was sent to earth by Etsaa to help people connect with nature and to teach them the path to enlightenment through the preparation and use of ayahuasca. Also, the condor.

chicha: A fermented drink made by Shuar women and the most important and sacred Shuar food.

datura: *Maikiua,* in Shuar. A psychotropic plant, one of the sacred teacher plants, along with ayahuasca (natem) and tobacco, that is taken for the purpose of journeying and seeing beyond the everyday world into the greater reality.

Etsaa: The sun; also the Shuar word for the legendary warrior who shapeshifted into the sun.

Evias: A legendary race of giant, white, cannibalistic monsters who live in the mountains and, according to story, have terrorized the Shuar.

Ewi: The Shuar god of the chonta palm and a measurement of time.

kakaram: An exceptionally brave warrior who possesses a great deal of arutam.

natem: *See* ayahuasca.

Nunqui: The goddess of the earth and of plants.

panqui: The spirit of the anaconda, or one who has arutam and shapeshifts into the anaconda or jaguar.

tsantsa: The head of an enemy that has been shrunk according to tradition and presented in a special ceremony. It is considered to be a sacred spirit and is treated with great respect.

tsentsak: Invisible darts that enter the heart as part of shamanic initiation. They are later used in healings by the shaman, helping him to look into a patient and see both where a problem originates and how it must be healed.

Tsunkqui: The first shaman, goddess of the waters.

tumank: A type of mouth harp made from a bowed bamboo branch and a "string" of monkey's gut.

tunduli: A hollow-log drum.

Tuntiak: The rainbow that lives in the sacred waterfall.

uwishin: One who knows, usually an elder.

Dream Change Coalition

 Inspired by the Shuar and other indigenous teachers, Dream Change Coalition is dedicated to: 1) changing the dream to a more earth-honoring and sustainable one, 2) preserving forests and other natural areas, and 3) using indigenous wisdom to foster environmental, social, and economic balance.

If you would like to:

- Order the Shuar CD or a POLE (Pollution Offset Lease for Earth) described in this book
- Visit the Shuar or other teachers in the Amazon and around the world
- Become a Dream Change Coalition member and help change the way we live to a more earth-honoring and sustainable one
- Learn about the World Dream Institute or Ayumpum Foundation
- Order books, audiotapes, or CDs by John Perkins and other DCC teachers

Please log on to:www.dreamchange.org or call (561) 622-6064

If you would like to make a tax-exempt contribution to Dream Change Coalition, Ayumpum Foundation, or the World Dream Institute, please make checks payable to **Dream Change*** and mail to:

Dream Change
P.O. Box 31357
Palm Beach Gardens, FL 33420

Other Books by John Perkins

- *Shapeshifting: Shamanic Techniques for Global and Personal Transformation*
- *Psychonavigation: Techniques for Travel Beyond Time*
- *The Stress-Free Habit: Powerful Techniques for Health and Longevity from the Andes, Yucatan, and the Far East*

**Dream Change is a 501 (c) 3 nonprofit corporation.*